DUXFORD TO KARACHI

DUXFORD TO KARACHI

An RAF Armourer's War

Fred Roberts

Victory Books

DUXFORD TO KARACHI: An RAF Armourer's War
© Fred Roberts, 2006.
ISBN: 0-9550431-8-2

First published 2006 by; -

Victory Books, PO Box 573, Worcester WR5 3WU, UK.
Tel: 07923 503105. Fax: 01905 767735.
www.victorybooks.co.uk   info@victorybooks.co.uk

Layout & design by Victory Books.
Printed & bound in the UK.

Contents

Foreword

Masses of literature has arisen out of the Second World War, including detailed academic campaign histories, the stories of particular battles, and, of course, the experiences of those who were there. Many prominent warriors, be they soldiers, sailors or airmen, published auto-biographies or had their biographies written after the war. The majority, however, had no platform or stage from which to recount their experiences, and so the greater number have gone unrecorded. As veterans have died, so their memories have passed with them, lost to history and future generations. We need to remember that war is not a glorious or wonderful thing, but a time of immeasurable suffering, violence and cruelty. This is why the recording of such memories is vital, because God forbid the day our world forgets how terrible wars are, and how ordinary folk suffer.

Fred Roberts came from a working class background and joined the RAF before the war broke out. This provided an opportunity for him to do and see things he would never otherwise have done, and likewise meet people of various standing with whom he would not have rubbed shoulders if not for the war. Fred, like countless others, did his 'bit', which included arming Spitfires in the Battle of Britain, during which he was bombed, and serving in the Far East, seperated from his new wife, Mary, and the normal life they both so longed to lead. Fred's is not an untypical tale, but it is unusual because so few 'ordinary' servicemen have committed their memories to paper, and for doing so I thank him. In this memoir of one man's war, we can look through a window onto the wartime RAF, both at home and in the Far East, and appreciate how the service ran, what made it tick. To build up a picture of what the wartime experience was all about, we don't just need tales of derring do, we also need to know what day-to-day life was like, how people lived, what were their priorities and how the war affected relationships and family life. We can get a good idea of these things from this book.

The war was, remember, an enormous interuption in normality, where the life of every individual was suddenly pledged to a higher cause; indeed, the individual had little or no control over his or her life, as Fred's story indicates. Having said that, the war years also represented an incredibly exciting time, especially for young men like Fred who worked on operational military aircraft like the Spitfire. All these years later, veterans can often still recall those far off days with great clarity - such was the impact of the time - but struggle to recall what they had for breakfast!

It is a very difficult task to commit one's memory to paper, and Fred should be commended for having done so; if only other veterans would follow his example before their experiences are lost forever.

I have known Fred and Mary Roberts for nearly 20 years, and have been grateful for their presence and support of numerous book signings and other events. It therefore gives me great pleasure to write this foreword and I can commend this book to you, the reader, without reservation.

Dilip Sarkar MBE, Worcester, January 2006.

Chapter One

WEST DRAYTON

There was no doubt in my mind that, providing they would have me, I was going to enlist in the Royal Air Force. On that day in October 1938 when I arrived outside the Plaza Cinema in Swansea I was not in the least interested in the posters telling of the week's silver screen attractions; my interest was in the posters displayed by the shop fronting the cinema: this was the RAF Recruiting Office, as it was then known.

The posters promised a trade, accommodation, clothes, good food, good pay, sport, and a good, healthy, life. I didn't hesitate, opening the door and stepping in to a warm welcome: a chair, a cigarette, and a friendly chat with a sergeant who appeared to be in charge. In fact, I only saw him and an airman in the office. I told them of my intention to join the RAF and that I considered my current job in the tin-plate industry to be a dead-end job: I was earning 18/3d (92p) per week, waiting perhaps years for promotion to 22/6d (£1.12p) per week, and all this in dirt, smoke and furnace heat with no job satisfaction whatsoever.

I was given the option of joining for six years. After a period of 'square bashing' at a Recruits' Training Centre I would then, I was told, go to a Technical Training School where there was a choice of trades on offer: Flight Mechanic Engines,

Flight Mechanic Airframes, Armourers, Electricians, Wireless Operators, and a host of others such as Cook and Butcher, Physical Training Instructor, Motor Driver etc. Or, I could sign on for seven years as an Aircraftman General Duties, re-mustering to a trade after completing the Recruit Training. Being undecided on a trade at that time, I took the second option and signed on for seven years.

I was then given a written examination, which took an hour or so, then filled in several forms. They told me that I would be sent a railway ticket and instructions, when and where to report in Cardiff for a medical examination. A few days later a letter arrived at home: I was to report to the RAF Recruiting Centre in Dominion Arcade, Queen Street, Cardiff. I duly passed the medical and informed that I would be accepted in the RAF. I was given my return railway ticket to Neath, and informed that I would be sent further instructions within a few days. These later arrived with a railway ticket; I was to report to Dominion Arcade on Monday, November 7th, 1938. With me I was instructed to take a change of under clothing, pyjamas, tooth-brush, soap, razor etc, two testimonials and my birth certificate. I was also told that I would then be going on from Cardiff to start my training.

Upon arrival at Cardiff on November 7th, I found that I was one of a party of eight, all seeking entry into the service. We were given a cursory medical examination and I remember one of our party being given 6d (2½p) and told to go out and buy himself a glass of beer because he couldn't provide the necessary liquid specimen. We were all subsequently proclaimed fit and healthy, and dismissed, being told to report back to the Centre at 1600 hours. Upon our return we were each given 2/6d (12½p) for our bed and breakfast, and were accompanied to Railway Street in Splott, a suburb of Cardiff, by the Commissionaire from the Centre who accommodated us all in his home, charging us our 2/6d. I remember him telling us that we could get an evening meal at the local fish and chip shop in the next street, at our own expense of course. This we enjoyed, eating from the newspaper wrapping under the lamp post outside the shop.

At about 0800 hours the following morning we departed from Cardiff by train to West Drayton. Someone came to Cardiff railway station to give the un-elected leader of our party our railway tickets and travel instructions, and a sealed package containing what we assumed was our enlisting papers. After a stop at Reading to change trains, and to have a meal of egg and chips at Lyons Corner House Restaurant, near the railway station, we arrived at West Drayton around 1430 hours. The RAF Station was only a few minutes walk and upon arrival we were immediately taken to the dining hall and given a cooked meal. After this we were conducted and allocated a bed. There were already a number of other potential airmen there who had arrived earlier from other parts of the country. For the next hour we were given a talk by an Airman, who appeared to be our guide and mentor, about the forthcoming proceedings. We were then taken to another building where we were crammed into a room with several hundred other bodies, all as eager as we to enlist. More form filling, there was so little room that I remember propping my forms against a wall to fill them in. It was at this early stage that we lost one of our Welsh colleagues: we had to declare any police records but he wouldn't do so. I believe that he had to return to Wales at his own expense, anyway we never saw him again.

We were then called, four at a time, into a small office where, bible in hand, we were sworn into the RAF, repeating an oath of allegiance to King and Country. Next we were given a number, mine being 625736, the Attesting Officer making it clear that the number would be an important factor throughout our RAF career, and so it proved to be: whatever one did or asked for, number, rank and name had first to be given and in that order.

After the Attestation Ceremony we passed from the office to a corridor where we were issued with a knife, fork and spoon, a one pint china mug and a towel, and told in no uncertain terms, by a sergeant with a loud voice, that these items were our personal property and that we would be responsible for them. Then those of the intake that he thought were in need of, and a few others that clearly didn't, were pushed along the corridor and into one of several booths with the barked instruction 'Haircut!' It was something like six cuts with the clippers up, and another around the back and sides to finish off.

Back to barrack block after this, we were told that there was a cold supper and cocoa in the dining hall should we need it, but most of us were too excited to eat. We also found that some of the other barrack blocks were also full of recruits being posted to various RAF Training Centres the next day. Together with another Welsh recruit, I duly found myself posted to RAF Uxbridge.

We were also introduced to the NAAFI (Navy, Army & Air Force Institute) Canteen, where I made my first NAAFI purchase, a writing pad with the RAF crest and a packet of envelopes which had the crest printed on the flap. In fact, this was the only crested paper I ever bought throughout my entire service.

The next morning I awoke at West Drayton with the realisation that I was now 625736 AC2 Roberts. This was November 9th, 1938, and we were soon to recognise our new status by the NCOs' tone of voice, so different from the previous evening now that we were all numbers! After our 0600 hours awakening, ablutions and breakfast we were all given a 'Free From Infection' (FFI) examination which entailed dropping our trousers and lifting up our shirts. There was a lot of embarrassment and flushed faces at this, given that the examining doctor was a young lady!

After this we gathered our belongings together and we two Welshmen joined 142 other recruits for a short coach journey to No 1 Recruits' Training Wing (RTW) at RAF Uxbridge. Where my other Welsh companions were posted I had no knowledge.

Chapter Two

UXBRIDGE

Through the gates at RAF Uxbridge we went, Camp Cinema on the left, Guard Room on the right, but where were the airfield and hangars? There weren't any, and this wasn't my idea of what the RAF was about. All I saw was a vast Parade Ground surrounded by large buildings which, I was later to learn, were the Dining Hall, NAAFI, and 10 barrack blocks, each with a name: Somme, Kut, Mons etc. We were to make our home of the next 10 weeks in Doiren Block. I was allocated Room 1 on the ground floor. The airmen in rooms 1 and 2 on the ground floor were designated No 1 Squad, 'J' Flight. All of us in No 1 Squad were to be offered Group 2 Technical Training Courses immediately following our Recruits' Training.

We were 24 airmen to a room, with six rooms in each Barrack Block. We 144 were soon to learn that the Senior NCO in charge of 'J' Flight was Sergeant Jordan, an Irishman: a right tartar on the square, but a really kind and fatherly figure in the Barrack Room. No 1 Squad's Junior NCO was Corporal Hancock, who was also Welsh, but this gave me no special treatment. My Welsh companion from Cardiff was billeted in a room on the second or third floor, being Nos 2 and 3 Squads respectively.

The remainder of that first day, I recall, was spent listening to Corporal Hancock giving us the programme for the next 10 weeks and warning us of the service's 'don'ts'. We also had inoculations and vaccinations for most known diseases, were shown how to make a bed 'service fashion', conducted to the Dining Hall and NAAFI, told of meal times, opening and closing times, reveille, and lights out times. There were no restrictions on the toilets, but we were warned of the PERIL of stepping on the Parade Ground (Square) at any time, day or night, except to parade.

Day two at Uxbridge was kitting out day. No 1 Squad was marched in some sort of order to the Clothing Store, where we were issued with our uniforms and all accompanying bits and pieces. The shorter of us were issued with one tunic open necked and one dog collared. The taller of the lads were issued with two tunics open necked. I believe we were among the last airmen to be issued with dog collared tunics. We were also issued with shirts, socks, boots, pants, vests, tie, cap field service, hat ceremonial, all the necessary bits of clothing, and a 'housewife' repair kit, containing needles, cotton, and other items required for clothing repair. Then there was that serviceman's enigma, Webbing. How we ever got it all together I don't know, but I do remember that when I hung my bayonet and water bottle on the finished item I concluded that the designer was a lunatic! I think we spent the rest of that day how to properly assemble the webbing, and how to produce a mirror finish on the toe caps of our boots.

On our third day we were kept to the barrack room until perhaps 1030 hours when we of 'J' Flight were marched onto the Square, where, in the company of all other Training Flights and the permanent staff, including the Commanding Officer and his officers, we participated in the Armistice Day Service, this being November 11th. This was my first parade on the Square. That afternoon we were visited in the barrack block by the camp tailor and his staff. We tried on our uniforms and had them marked for alterations, a bit taken in here, a bit out there, a bit off the bottom. They were taken away and returned a couple of days later, suitably altered.

It was during those first days that I made my first friend in the RAF, a Scot from Fife named Jamie Stuart, though I always knew him as 'Sandy'. We became the best of friends throughout the 10 weeks of our training. I also made a friendship with a London East-ender called Johnnie Andrews; we were together until July 1939, when we were posted as Armourers to different squadrons.

Metal stamps were loaned to us and we were instructed to stamp our service numbers on our cutlery, brushes, and anything else we could stamp. We had to stud the leather soled boots we were issued with, the other pair being rubber soled; the studded boots were worn for work and marching, rubber soles for walking out. We were also told to buy a tin of 'Blanco' whitener each from the canteen, and blanco our webbing and ceremonial belts.

Having received our uniforms back from the tailors, suitably altered, we started our drill training: "Fall in, tallest on the right, shortest on the left. Right Dress! Number from the right, form fours. Right-turn. Quick march! Slow March! About turn!" We had to quickly learn our right from left feet. Then came Rifle Drill, and on the couple of occasions I dropped my rifle I found that I had other names not given by my parents! Hancock knew them, and funnily enough a few other lads in No 1 Squad were endowed with the same names! One of the Squad caused the collapse of a whole line of piled rifles by accidentally knocking the end pile with his foot; he was told that he wasn't whosoever he thought he was, and was asked by Sergeant Jordan, who was taking the whole 'J' Flight parade that day, if he had enlisted because his parents' didn't want him!

We also suffered a full Kit Lay-out and Kit Inspection, and Uniform Parade ever Thursday before Pay Parade. Our kit was laid out on our beds as per a photograph supplied, aided by Corporal Hancock the first few times. We stood to attention at our beds, complete with ceremonial belts blanco'd and brass buckles and buttons polished, awaiting the arrival of the Officer in charge (i/c) 'J' Flight, accompanied by Sergeant Jordan. They walked around the beds, between then missing nothing, and made suitable comments if things were not just right.

We were very fortunate in No 1 Squad in that we had Corporal Hancock as our Junior NCO, as a number of lads in No 3 Squad had their beds tipped over on different occasions, just prior to inspection, by their sadistic corporal who took a perverse delight in seeing them in trouble. He was the only man I met throughout my entire RAF career who ever resorted to bullying.

One evening during our first week, a fellow room mate went berserk, smashing his head against the wall and screaming. It frightened all of us, being inexperienced in this kind of behaviour. Some of the bigger lads restrained him until the Medical Staff took him away. We were told that he had some kind of vaccine fever, and never saw him again.

Sometimes we talked of home, but were never homesick. There was so much to occupy our time, so much to learn and do, all the polishing and blancoing of kit, barrack room duties, such as fire-place cleaning and floor polishing. We were each responsible for polishing our own bed space and portion of floor from the foot of our bed to the centre of the room. Then there was ablution cleaning, inside window cleaning, dusting, I could go on! Of course there was a roster and a change of duties every week. I can't remember having much time for the NAAFI before 2030 hours on any evening whilst I was at Uxbridge, and it was lights out at 2200 hours.

It was a cold winter. We were issued with one scuttle of coal per room a night, which barely lasted until lights out, and in any case we were not allowed to light the fire until 1700 hours. Hot water was also in short supply, there were occasions when we shared a bath only a third full of water.

My bed was one of four nearest the fire, there being two, one each side of the barrack room. These four beds were always the gathering point around the fire for the spit and polish session every evening, and the other three lads and I holding these four beds were always in friendly conflict with the rest because we couldn't sit or lay on our beds in comfort. But there was one advantage: we four always had a warm bed to put our feet in at lights out!

End of week four and, hurrah, we were to be allowed out of camp after 1300 hours on Saturday. We had been confined to barracks since enlisting, I suppose we were deemed unfit to be presented to the general public until we had four weeks discipline instilled in us. Only then would we be considered smart enough to grace the pavements of Uxbridge High Street. Reflecting upon it, I suppose that the locals had seen it all before.

Before being allowed out of barracks we were marched one squad at a time to the Prophylactic Room at the rear of the Main Guard Room, and there were told about the dangers of associating with local 'Ladies of the Night' (and afternoon, come to that!). We were showed how, should we make use of these services, how to use the cream or other venereal disease preventatives stored for that purpose in the Prophylactic Room. We were also told about condoms, and that these could purchased at high street chemists.

This particular Sunday we were also included in the Church Parade to Uxbridge church, just across the road from the barracks. If I remember rightly, it was march around the Square then out through the main gates, led by the Central Band of the RAF, which also accompanied the church organist. After the service we were marched back on the Square and dismissed. I am sure we thought ourselves the equal of any Guards regiment, we had our shoulders back, heads held high and were certainly proud of ourselves.

Wednesday afternoon was Sports Afternoon. There was Association Football, rugby football or cross country running. I chose running the first Wednesday, but Hancock didn't tell us that the course was about eight miles across Hillington Common! After that my sport became Association Football, which we played in our studded boots.

We each had a small steel locker bolted to the wall above our beds, in which to store our clothes and personal belongings. Our clothes were folded and stacked as per a photograph with top clothing on one shelf, under clothing on the other shelf, but personal belongings, such as writing paper or photographs, were hidden out of sight. We each also had a small wooden bedside locker on which we kept our toilet accessories, mug, cutlery and boots. Webbing and rifle were hung on pegs behind our beds.

I soon found out how to keep creases in my trousers, there being no electric sockets for irons. This I did by applying toilet soap to the inside crease using a shaving brush, then stretching the trousers on top of my three mattresses (or 'Biscuits' as they were called in the service). The trousers were placed under the bottom blanket and sheet, and I then slept on them. The biscuits were three to a bed, about 2 feet six inches square, and during the day were arranged to become a kind of easy chair: the biscuits were placed to form a seat and back-rest, my sheets, blankets and bolster going behind the back-rest.

We had all gotten to know each other well enough after a few weeks to start leg-pulling and practical jokes. These were mostly carried out on a Saturday night when the lads returned to a dark room after an evening in town. Apple-pie beds and the sewing up of one pyjama leg were regular pranks, and near Christmas a handful of prickly holly pushed into someone's bed was popular. Another favourite was fixing the bed so that when the victim pushed his way between the sheets the bed would collapse in the middle, the occupant finishing up on the floor. There were times, though, when the joke misfired, the victim having had a drink or two and just slept where he lay, oblivious to the fact that he had been floored! Mostly, though, these pranks ended with the victim's language waking up the whole room!

Very rarely did anyone go out of a week-day evening, we had very little money and even less spare time, besides we were too tired after a day on the Square. Saturday we all went out either to Uxbridge or walked to Southall. Some of the lads came back boasting of success with local girls, but we were only there for a few weeks and as they were so used to the RAF that most would have nothing to do with us.

We were told that we were to be taught Aircraft Handling, and excitedly debated which airfield we would be taken to. Northolt was favourite as it was closest, but were we in for a shock: Uxbridge held two old Bristol Fighters (minus wings) in a brick building where they were fixed to the floor. Our Aircraft Handling experience consisted of learning how to start the engine by swinging the propeller, under the overall charge of a Sergeant Fitter, and another fitter or flight mechanic sat in the cockpit, controlling the engine. Only the tallest of us were actually allowed to swing the prop, we shorties had to be content to take our turn sitting on the machine's tail, whilst the engine was run at full revs. Our heads were nearly blown off, but little did we realise that this would be our norm when posted to squadrons!

Another experience we underwent was being shut in a gas chamber whilst it was filled with tear gas, respirators on. Then we were made to remove our masks and run through the chamber, a tearful experience indeed. This was to demonstrate the respirator's efficiency and to show us the result of exposure to one of the less evil gasses. Down at the Rifle Butts we were given instructions on rifle shooting, and I became rather good at this, probably because I had a lot of experience firing air guns. Most of my colleagues were also good after a few trial rounds.

Just before Christmas, the whole of 'J' Flight was put on fatigues for a week, something every Uxbridge trainee suffered. This meant duties in the Kitchen, Dining Hall, cleaning around the camp as directed and a host of other chores. I spent a day as Orderly Room Runner in the RTW Orderly Room, being required to sit in best blue in the Orderly Room annex, awaiting instructions. Every time an officer entered the room I leapt to attention and saluted, but fortunately didn't make the mistake of saluting a Warrant Officer! One of the errands I ran was to take a message to the Sergeants' Mess but no-one told me that corporals and airmen (the lowest form of life) were only welcome at the back door of both Sergeants' and Officers' Messes. I therefore committed the ultimate sin by walking through the front door, which was the biggest mistake I made in my entire career! I can't remember exactly what was bawled at me, but it wasn't complimentary, and I must have broken some kind of speed record in executing my retreat! Fortunately just around the corner I met another sergeant who had not witnessed my blunder, and in response to my inquiry as to where the message should be delivered, he directed me to the rear of the Mess. Two of the Fatigue Days I remember spending in the Tin Room, this entailing scraping and scrubbing out baking tins; there were hundreds of them and it was filthy, hard, work, as unlike those in the Plate Room we had no mechanical aids. I finished the week cleaning the floor and wiping down tables in the NAAFI, which was good as we had free tea and buns!

Christmas 1938 brought with it five days leave, from Christmas Eve until December 28th. We paid for and got our rail tickets in the Dining Hall at Service Rates, on the afternoon of December 23rd, so that we could get away early the next day. But what a disappointment going home to Neath transpired to be. All of my old work mates seemed to be people I had known in the past but no longer had anything in common with, and they seemed to think that I was somehow above them, which was ridiculous seeing as my feet (using a pun) had yet to leave the ground. In spite of my family's warm and loving welcome I soon became bored, and returned to Uxbridge on the first train out of Neath on December 27th, 24 hours earlier than I had to.

By January we were beginning to look forward to our forthcoming Passing Out Parade and to our subsequent Posting. We had snow both over and since Christmas but this did not delay our progress, and we now considered ourselves well disciplined and trained. We could dress, march and salute well enough to please our NCO instructors, and with good food, regular training and PT, I am sure that we were all fitter than we ever had been before. The great day dawned and there were about 140 of us with a section of the Central Band playing for us. We went through our whole drill procedure in front of the RTW CO, Wing Commander Gold: we quick marched, slow marched, sloped arms, ordered arms, we went through the whole routine, being on the Square for 60 – 70 minutes. Afterwards congratulations were in order, one final room and kit inspection and we were passed out ready for posting. Next day we were instructed to remove the studs from our boots as we wouldn't be allowed to work on aircraft wearing them. Then we were all held in suspense for a few hours, deliberately I think by Hancock as a leg-pull before being given our postings as he had them all morning. These ranged over a number of RAF stations: eight of us, including myself, were posted to No 1 Air Armanent School, RAF Manby, Lincolnshire, we having all chosen to be trained as Armourers. Where was Manby? Out came the maps, what town was it near? Our NCO hadn't even heard of it (upon arrival we discovered that it was a new station which had only opened the previous June).

Next it was off to have the occupants of Room 1 photographed in a group, the photographs being signed by each of us. Our posting date was Friday, 13th January, 1939; was that an omen? It was goodbye to Uxbridge, with which we had all shared a love, hate relationship. Uxbridge recruits are always proud to say "I was trained at No 1 RTW", where, it is said, the service would make or break a man.

Chapter Three

MANBY

A voice from the semi-darkness, "Willoughby, change here for Sutton-on-Sea and Maplethorpe", but who wants to visit the seaside in January? We were advised to get off the train if we wanted to get to Grimoldby and wait there for the local branch train which would arrive in a few minutes. I was bitterly cold on that platform, nothing I had known in Wales had been as cold, and I was both hungry and thirsty to boot. The kitchen staff at Uxbridge supplied us with rations which consisted of two one inch thick slices of bread and a slab of cheese, plus an apple, and this had been eaten before we got to Peterborough. Unfortunately there were no instructions with the brown paper bag of mixed tea and sugar, and the two tins of carnation milk that had been issued to our party we gave to an old lady on the underground train en route to Kings Cross. In fact our last drink had been a cup of tea in the buffet car there, and that was now hours before.

We did, however, have a little excitement on the journey. Somewhere near Boston, Paddy Davidson called us to the corridor: there was a plane, a Hawker Hart or Hind, flying alongside the train then overtaking, circling around and repeating the manoeuvre. This was done several times, there being a lot of hand waving between ourselves and the aircrew, this being our first involvement with an actual aeroplane!

I can't remember the names of all the boys posted to Manby with me, but my friend John Andrews was there. Sandy Stuart had chosen an electricians course and so had gone to Electricians' School. There was Les Neville, who had been our right marker at Uxbridge, John O'Connor, Albert Irons and, of course, little Paddy Davidson who had come all the way from Ireland and was the shortest of us all.

By the time we arrived at Grimoldby it was completely dark. I think the station was illuminated by a couple of oil lamps, it was raining heavily and to all of us it was even colder. "No, they never supply transport!" the Porter replied in answer to our question, "Youm will har to walk, s'about a moile down that road, past the pub and café, o'er the cross roads then youm will see the rows of lights of the buildings. Loike a town it is!" So off we trudged, getting wetter with every stride, no lights until we got to the pub and then it was only a light over a door or an illuminated window. To me this was utter desolation, but soon we could see the rows of light in distant barrack blocks, 'Keep going lads', I thought, 'we'll soon be there!'

At last we reached the Guard Room and a friendly reception and promise of a hot meal in 15 minutes! After Neville had given in our posting papers to the Sergeant MP, we were conducted from there first to a barrack block, to a third floor room, where we dumped our kit. The room was already partly occupied, but we were not given time for introductions, it was straight to the Dining Hall. The Guard Room had called through and a mixed grill awaited us with hot tea, more of both if we wanted it. I don't know if the Duty Cook had a kind heart or just wanted to impress us, but it was absolute luxury.

Back in the barracks block we all introduced ourselves. The other occupants had arrived earlier that day from other RTWs and we were all to join the same Armourers' Course. We 'Uxbridge Eight' sorted ourselves out and selected a bed each before unpacking our kit bags, putting our clothes and other kit away.

A corporal arrived and introduced himself. He was from the Administration Office and was on Permanent Staff. He informed us that we were all a part of No 7 Armament Course and that our Course NCO would be Flight Sergeant Fisher, whom we would meet next morning. He would be giving us all the information about our future, and we were to make ourselves comfortable as we would be in that room for two weeks, until, that was, all 66 men on the course could be accommodated in one block. Also, there were some more trainees like ourselves expected to arrive and take up the remaining beds, making us a total of 22 in the room. Finally we were told that breakfast was at 0730 hours and afterwards we were to parade again on the Square at 0845 hours, but were to keep ourselves out of sight until then. I made up my bed, the blankets, sheets and bolster were already there, then I had time to sit and reflect, and discuss the room and Manby with my new room mates who had seen it in daylight. What a difference to Uxbridge! Here we were in a new building just six months old with central heating, six feet high steel wardrobes and a bed side locker, highly polished flooring and all the hot water required for showers and baths. What more eye openers would we find over the next few days, I wondered? Most of my fellow room mates had already tasted these luxuries elsewhere, but we from Uxbridge had only known the delights of Doiren Block!

Chapter Four

No 7 ARMAMENT COURSE

Our introduction to Manby: -

"My name is Flight Sergeant Fisher, and I will be your N.C.O for the duration of this course. We are going to be together for the next six months, so I hope we can all be the best of friends and work together as a team with the minimum of trouble, to achieve good results at the end of the course."

That was how Flight Sergeant Fisher introduced himself to us that Saturday, January 14th, 1939. The whole course, all 66 airmen were present on the square, but temporarily we were split among different barrack blocks until No 1 Course, who were taking their final examinations the following week, were posted away. Then we would be all billeted together in block T3, in the rooms they would vacate. We were formed up in fours, Neville again being our right marker, being the tallest, and we were marched to the Main Armament School building. In the Lecture Hall Flight Sergeant Fisher, or 'Flight' as he instructed us to address him, told us the course would be over a period of six months. The course would be divided into two periods with a written examination at the end of the first period and both a written and practical examination at the end of the course.

We would be in classes of 11 airmen per class, he would be the only serving instructor, all the other instructors would be ex-servicemen and the instructors would be teaching, so far as I can remember, as follows:

No 1 Rifle, Revolver, Signal Pistol, Browning Machine Gun

No 2 Vickers Gas Operated Machine Gun, Lewis Machine Gun

No 3 Vickers Recoil Machine Gun, Synchronisation Gear, Scarff Rings

No 4 Bomb Carriers, Bombs, Bomb Fuses, Bomb Pistols, Flares.

No 5 Workshop Practices.

No 6 Bomb Sights, Gun Sights, Explosives, Ammunition.

This last, No 6, was Flight Sergeant Fisher's subjects. He also told us that we were his first trainees and ours was his first course; he was married and lived in the Married Quarters, and would be available to us night or day should we be in need of advice. Fisher was to be both father and mother to us for the duration of our stay at Manby.

We were separated into six classes of 11 men, I can't remember what determined the division into classes, but I was placed into class No 2. There were three of us from Uxbridge in class No 2, Neville, Paddy Davidson and myself.

We made out pass cards that we were required to carry every time we left camp, and authorised our being out of camp until 2359 hrs. These were taken away to be signed and deposited in the Guard Room, from where we drew them on leaving camp and deposited them on our return. Then we had an hour or more of questions and answers. The Flight told us he was a Fitter Armourer, and an ex-Apprentice, and after satisfying our curiosity on all aspects of the course we were dismissed for the remainder of the week-end with the instructions to parade outside Block U2, the block I was in, at 0745hrs the following Monday morning, and also to keep out of sight Sunday morning while the Church Parade was ongoing.

I can't remember anyone from our room leaving camp that Saturday or Sunday, firstly we had little money, secondly we were quite comfortable in our centrally heated rooms and well-fed. What more did any of us want? Besides, it was too bloody cold to want to explore Lincolnshire in January!

Monday morning, and we had our first experience of a person who we were to know in the future as the 'Chicken', on account of his long beaky nose, an ugly-looking corporal from the Station Warrant Officer's staff, who, every other week as part of his duties as Orderly Corporal, charged around the barrack blocks at 0600hrs, screaming, blowing a bugle (he couldn't play it), running up and down the stairs, threatening the late risers with a jug of water. We newcomers were terrified of him, not knowing he wouldn't dare actually throw the water over us, but it did ensure that we were all in time for breakfast.

All the station personnel except those on duty and those on sick parade, paraded on the square at 0800 hrs every weekday morning for a short Church Service and the raising of the Royal Air Force flag. After this, on our first Monday, we were marched again to the Main Lecture Hall, where we were given a talk by the School Commanding Officer, this was a repeat of what we had already been told by the Flight, but he added that the Station also included an Air Gunnery School, and a Bombing School, and controlled the Bombing and Gunnery Ranges at Theddlethorpe, which we would visit as part of our course; there was also a Senior N.C.O's Armament Course running at Manby.

The C.O informed us that the aircraft we would see flying from Manby were Hawker Harts and Hawker Hinds, Westland Wallaces and Fairy Gordens, the latter two types being used for drouge towing, that is an air-towed moving target for air firing practice. There was also an ancient Bolton and Paul Overstrand, and I think the odd Gloster Gauntlet and Hawker Fury.

Then we were taken to our classrooms which, in No 7 Course's case, were in a wooden annexe building adjacent to the main school building. This, the Flight said, was excellent as we weren't under the scrutiny of the Commissioned staff as we would have been in the main building. The workshop was in a separate building near to the annexe.

After being introduced to our Civilian Instructors, we started our training. I still remember that my first subject was the Vickers Gas Operated Machine Gun, more commonly known as the Vickers K Gun. Our first class in the afternoon was on gun sights with the Flight. It was also our first lesson in guile. The Flight didn't possess a watch of his own so he sent one of our number to the school stores for a Bomb Sight Mk something. This came in a box with, of all things, a watch. The Bomb Sight remained on loan to the course for a few weeks, then returned to the stores in the morning and another collected in the afternoon. Our Flight Sergeant always had the right time and it proved there was no point in him buying a timepiece.

RAF Manby turned out to be a wonderful place after our previous experience. The rooms were so warm, despite the east coast winds outside, and the opportunity to shower every day or to soak in a full bath of water by oneself was luxury. The food was excellent and ample, no thoughts of having to supplement it in the NAAFI, and we were a good 22 airmen in our room. Flight Sergeant Fisher saw we had everything that we needed.

It was classrooms Monday to Friday, two subjects each morning and another two subjects in the afternoon. All literature on each subject was supplied at the beginning of the course. This became our own property. In our workshop practices we were set the task of making an article that had no use of any kind but contained all the elements of metalwork, i.e. sawing, filing, drilling, thread tapping, brazing, soldering and wire beading. This work was planned to coincide with the completion of the course and could be judged as part of the final examination.

After a couple of weeks we were all moved into T3 Block, vacated by No 1 Course, and we occupied the two ground floor rooms and one second floor room; I was in Room 2 along with John Andrews. Except for the classrooms we were managing to stay together. John and I had also made our fist venture into Louth, the local town, but I remember I didn't think a lot of it being winter and dark early I don't suppose I gave much time or thought to sightseeing. I found later in the year, however, that there was a lot of beautiful countryside around Manby.

We travelled into town on a local bus that ran from the camp gates to Louth for the RAF, and it was 6d each way fare, the last bus back to camp leaving Louth at 2200 hrs. If that was missed it was a four mile walk but no Forms 252 were raised providing one got back within a half-hour after midnight. There were often too many people for the last bus.

Pay Parade was held on Thursday in the Main School Building. There I lined up, stepped forward, saluted, gave my number, "Sir, 625736 Roberts", saluted again, picked up the 12/-, about turned and marched off back to the classroom. We also did Guard Duties or Fire Picket Duties about one night a month. We were informed of these duties on Daily Routine Orders (DROs), which we had to read daily as one never knew when a duty came up. They were posted in an alphabetical rota. For this, one reported to the Guard Room at 1745 hrs in best blue uniform and overcoat, ceremonial hat and belt. After inspection by the Orderly Sergeant and Orderly Officer we were allocated guard posts around the station. Some of the posts were patrols in pairs, such as the Hangar Patrol or the

Barrack Block Patrol, while others were single guard posts, such as Main Gate and Officers' Gate. We carried these duties out on a two hours on, four hours off rota. Fire Picket was a doddle, all one did was sleep in the Fire Picket Room opposite the Guard Room!

I believe I did two Church Parades in my six months at Manby. The village church was small, so only a few personnel were called on each Sunday as room had to be left for the locals. When we were detailed to attend we dressed in best blue and marched the mile to the Church.

Every Saturday morning we had a room inspection. There were no classes. This inspection was taken by an officer accompanied by Flight Sergeant Fisher. For this inspection we lined all the beds up and the floor was polished to a mirror finish. This was accomplished by making great use of the bumper, a long handled wooden block with a thick lead base to give it weight and polishing rags underneath. This bumper was pushed to and fro over the floor to attain the necessary shine, sometimes having one of our room mates stand on the bumper to give additional weight. Also, all our sheets and blankets had to be correctly folded on the bed and our clothes tidily stored in the wardrobe.

Periodically we had a full kit inspection with our full kit laid out as we did weekly at the RTW. For both these weekly and periodical inspections we stood by our beds at attention in our best blue. After these inspections were over we were free until Monday morning parade, unless we were detailed for duties or Church Parade.

The weeks were passing and I was really enjoying my life, more than I ever thought possible. The period I spent slaving in the tin plate rolling mills had already disappeared into the back of my mind and I was also beginning to forget the poor standard of living that I knew prior to joining the RAF. I looked forward to school more every day. I thoroughly enjoyed the classes. Every one of the instructors made their subjects so interesting, the Flight being the best by adding little anecdotes to his lecture from his experiences as an armourer, thus making the talk both interesting and amusing.

Guns and Gun Sights became my favourite subjects. Guns were something I could dismantle and assemble with my hands and didn't have to think a lot about. I even found the theory of gun sights such as the Ring and Bead sight, or the Norman Vane sight and the Reflector sight easy and interesting. But I could never grasp anything to do with Bomb Sights. I could never get the hang of airspeeds, groundspeeds, windspeeds, drift and heights and all the other paraphernalia that went with bombing.

It was March when we visited the Bombing Range at Theddlethorpe. I remember we went two classes at a time with the Flight. This was our practical lesson in the chain of an explosion. This was done using a live 20lb 1914 - 1918 vintage Cooper bomb, a 1lb slab of gun cotton and a fulminate of Mercury electric detonator. The lesson went off with a BANG! We also had a demonstration of slow burning fuse and fast burning fuse, and were taken to the Bombing Range Marker building where we had explained to us the method of plotting the practice bombing on the targets. I still to this day don't understand why we flew a red flag over the range while we were preparing the explosion, then lowering it and flying a green flag while the explosion was taking place.

We spent a few periods on the Bombing Simulator, where conditions were created as per a Bombing Aircraft. My target on my Bombing run was Portsmouth Naval Dockyard, but although I'm certain I had the Ark Royal in the Bomb sight when I pressed the button, the cross marking the spot where the bombs landed was somewhere in Ryde on the Isle of Wight. Someone must have moved the island! Still, some of the lads dropped their bombs on Portsmouth town and I remember one even bombed the New Forest. The Royal Navy needed to have no fear of us!

I heard that if I hurried up to the hangars straight after inspection on a Saturday morning and drew a chest type parachute from the Parachute Store, then hang about around the Watch Tower looking interested in everything going on, I might be lucky enough to be invited over by one of the ground crews working on one of the aircraft on the tarmac, or even on of the pilots and offered the opportunity to have a flight. This I did the following Saturday. I couldn't get anyone else from my room interested so it was a solo effort on my part. I stood on the tarmac for about an hour complete with parachute and harness, I had been shown how to wear it in the store. There were about 10 of us altogether, then I was the fourth or fifth to be beckoned, it was just pot luck, but I was invited to take a flight in the rear of a Hawker Hind. I was nervous. Should I refuse? I had never been in an aeroplane before. Indeed, I had never been higher than 20 feet off the ground!

I was up and into the plane in just a few seconds, assisted by the Flight Rigger who showed me how to secure the Monkey Tail which fastened the harness to the floor of the plane. I had nothing to fear, I thoroughly enjoyed the flight. It was just straight flying and lasted about 40 minutes. The pilot, a sergeant, told me afterwards, when I told him it was my first flight and thanked him, that we had flown over Grimsby and Cleethorpes, then down the cost to Maplethorpe, then inland before returning to Manby. I had plenty to talk about when I returned to the Barrack Room. I think I bored them all stiff. This was the first of many Saturday morning flights I made at Manby. Sometimes, when there were fewer lads looking for flights, it was possible to get a couple of flights. We were warned by the Parachute Packers that should we open the parachute accidentally or otherwise it would cost us 2/6d to have it repacked. This applied to everyone including aircrew, dead or alive!

Easter was coming and we were told that we could have five days leave and a free rail ticket and our Credits. These Credits consisted of the 2/- that was taken from our 14/- pay every week and saved for us, plus the 1/7d or 1/9d we were allowed for uniform, toothpaste, polish, etc every week and which was paid every quarter. But before leave we had to sit our first period examination. This was for three days and covered all we had been taught, excluding workshop practices. I did well on all the papers except, as I knew, my bomb sight paper was rubbish. The subject was beyond me! We were to have the results when we returned from leave.

I really didn't want to go on leave. I would have been happy to have stayed at Manby over the Easter period. I still had the Christmas leave experience in mind, but by this time we had been in the RAF long enough to warrant permission to wear civilian clothes when off duty so all the lads were going home to collect their suits, blazers, flannels and striped shirts, etc and that was the only reason I returned to Wales.

Chapter Five

No 7 ARMAMENT COURSE

The Final Period

That short Easter break passed very quickly. I remember meeting a few of my old work mates and school friends. The main topic was always 'what is it like in the RAF, did I like it, did I do any flying?' Of course I couldn't let the opportunity pass to tell them of my Saturday morning flights, enlarging on the tales every time! I think there was doubt in their minds but it never bothered me. I'm sure I was happier in my life than they were in theirs.

It was nice to see my family, my brother and sisters seemed to have grown six inches since I saw them at Christmas, everyone was pleased to have me at home, but I wasn't settled, my life had changed so much I was glad when I was on the train to Paddington.

About a dozen of us of No 7 Course met up at Kings Cross to get the Grimsby train. I and a few more were in uniform, carrying our civilian clothes in our cases, but who were these odd looking fellows in suits and sports clothing who came across to us? We hardly recognised them, an unfamiliar change of dress does alter the appearance of even one's best friends. Among other topics of discussion between us on the train, the subject of civilian clothes arose and it was agreed that there would be a lot more of our course members who would need to be identified when we met them at Peterborough and Louth.

On our first Monday back at Manby we were given our exam results, and of course, as I expected my paper on bomb sights was a flop but I was doing well on all the other subjects that is until we met our Browning Gun Instructor. I can see him now, his waxed army sergeant major moustache was fairly bristling, his words "The whole course, yes the whole bloody lot of you, your papers on Browning Gun weren't awful they were bloody!", really screaming the words at us. We did have sympathy from the Flight, he was quick to side with us and pointed out that the army were always ready to criticise the other services and to panic when thing didn't go as they thought right. The course carried on, Vickers Recoil, 800 rounds per minute, Vickers K Gun 1000 rounds per minute, Browning Gun 1100 rounds per minute, 50lb GP bombs, 250lb SAP bombs, 500lb AP bombs, parachute flares. We had all this and a lot more to learn by July so there was no respite. I could now dismantle and assemble rifles, revolvers and machine guns in my sleep.

I had better mention some of my room mates. There was John Andrews, my particular friend and a former crane driver on the East London Docks; his stories of how boxes of tea and sacks of sugar, plus other commodities, fell from the crane to the ground while being hoisted from the ships made good listening. Of course, as John said, the goods were in such a damaged state they couldn't be sent onto the consignees, what could be done with the stuff? Today one would say it 'fell off the back of a lorry'. Then we had a fellow about 30 years of age, his surname was Greenwood and pre-joining. He did car interior designing for Rolls Royce, visiting prospective customers and then designing the interiors as per their requirements. He did a lot of paintings of his ideas of cars during the evenings and they were wonderful, years before their time. I believe he joined the RAF because of wife trouble at home. There was also a fellow whose name I have forgotten, but who worked for one of the big pharmaceutical companies prior to enlisting and he used to purchase the ingredients somewhere and make a hair cream similar to Brylcream in the room fire bucket! This he sold to course members at 3d for a 1lb jam jar full. I could go on about more of the chaps, but suffice it to say that we had a wonderful cross section of people and some real characters.

About this time we had an Air Ministry directive put on our notice board asking for volunteers to re-muster and go on a Balloon Operator's Course at RAF Cardington, near Bedford. I think this was at the forming of Balloon Command. We had a lot of discussion about it in our room because it was suggested that to get in on the ground floor might lead to early promotion. Finally none of us took the opportunity, but one of the lads in another room volunteered and left us. I believe his home was in Luton, which was the attraction.

The weather was warming up now and the evenings lengthening. Although we hadn't any time to explore the local countryside on weekday evenings, as we were too busy swotting or room cleaning, we did go out on Saturday afternoons and evenings to Louth with perhaps a visit to the cinema or a pint in one of the pubs in town. Sunday became the chief day out for John and me, and the venue usually Maplethorpe or Sutton-on-Sea. Because of the lack of trains, none on a Sunday and no buses, we had to hitch hike. This wasn't difficult as a lot of airmen from Manby made for the same resorts. There was lot of traffic on the road, mostly day trippers from the Lincoln and Nottingham areas. Although mostly in civilian clothes, I think we must have been recognised as RAF because we were usually asked by the kind people that picked us up if we were stationed at Manby.

The attraction at these seaside resorts were the girls. There seemed to be hundreds of them all on their annual week-long holiday. There they were in their Bed and Breakfasts, or Holiday chalets, we didn't have to give them the wink as they chatted *us* up! They mostly seemed to think that because we were in the RAF we were all flying personnel. We didn't like to tell them different, we did enjoy relating to them our fictitious experiences at the controls of fighters and bombers (shooting the line)! All we got for our efforts was any number of close encounters, but not nearly as close as one would have got in the war years, just a few years later. Our difficulty, though, was getting back to Manby on a Sunday evening. All the lads started back about the same time but the trippers didn't, so we often walked miles on the road before we got a lift.

I was progressing well on the course, bomb carriers and Scarf rings and synchronisation gear were now added to our syllabus and my workshop piece was progressing well. I was still really enjoying everything. Practical jokes in the barrack room were an every weekend item and we were always thinking up new stunts to pull on a Saturday night on the late arrivals back from town.

Whitsun was with us, the time had flown by and another long weekend off duty. John had gone off to his home in London but I stayed at Manby. I couldn't afford the train fare anywhere but I did take a 295 (Leave Form), should I need to stay out of camp after midnight.

I can't remember where we borrowed the bicycles but one of my fellow room mates (his name has gone) and I got hold of these bikes on the Whit Monday morning and he suggested that we cycled to Cleethorpes. His home was in the Nottingham area and he had been to Cleethorpes on holidays in the past. We set off; 22 miles each way, we had plenty of energy and more time, so we had a pleasant day there but it was no different to Maplethorpe, just bigger. We left about 1930 hrs but had no lights on our bikes and so were allowing ourselves ample time to get back before dark.

Cycling through Grimsby we overtook two young ladies walking, and on looking back over my shoulder at them one of them smiled. What a beautiful smile! I was attracted and stopped. My colleague was anxious to get on, but I told him to carry on if he so wished but he waited. I let the young ladies catch up and spoke. The beautiful smiler was quite willing to chat. We stayed there talking for, I suppose, 15 minutes. I explained our hurry to get back to Manby. She said she understood and we made arrangements to meet on the second Sunday after that day at the Bus Station in Grimsby. She told me her name was Edna Mold and asked that I come in uniform to prove that I was in the RAF. My 295 weekend pass wasn't enough. It was a long time after that that she told me the reason she wanted me in uniform that first date was to show me off to her friends should we meet any of them.

We got back to Manby alright but I remember we had to dismount and wheel the bikes every time anything approached or overtook us the last few miles, as we didn't want to be in the local Police Court for not having any lights.

It was back to work after the holiday. More bombs, guns and explosives. Now we were well into synchronisation gear, where the guns were timed to fire through the arc of the propeller without hitting the propeller blades. Our Instructor on this subject also taught us Vickers Recoil Machine Gun, and I remember him well because the third subject he taught was Gun Gauges, but he always spelled it "gagues"; no matter how many times we corrected it on the blackboard the next time it was "gagues" again!

I was given a Fire Picket duty one Saturday after Whitsun and Saturday Guard and Fire Picket duties were always 1200 hrs Saturday until 0600 hrs on Sunday. That Saturday afternoon we were relaxing in the Picket Room, stretched out on the beds when a lady came running from the Officers' Married Quarters screaming "Fire! Fire!" We six pickets jumped off our beds and dashed outside. We grabbed up the handcart containing the standpipe and hosepipe, and charged off up the road to the scene of the fire. Bearing in mind that we had not received any instructions of any kind, it was out with the hosepipe and standpipe, connect them up to the hydrant, which we found quite easy. Two of the lads were carrying the hose and nozzle and were into the house and halfway up the stairs when one of our 'Fred Carno's' squad turned on the water. I wasn't in the house to see it, but it must have been hilarious. It was chaotic like a Charlie Chaplin film, two boys were knocked back down the staircase, through the hall into the sitting room and kitchen, and then out through the front door, but no water in the bedroom where the fire was! Eventually after about five minutes of chaos, we did get more organised, got things under control and put out the fire, but I'm sure we did the major portion of the damage.

Apparently the officer living in the house had his mother, an old lady, staying there with him and his wife; the old lady had gone to sleep in the chair in her bedroom and dropped some knitting onto the electric fire, which was alight, and this was the cause of the blaze. She was lucky, she woke up and escaped before the flames really took hold. We too, were lucky as we didn't get charged for causing so much water damage, in fact, we were congratulated on our prompt and quick turn out!

I kept that date with Edna Mold and at first we were quite shy of each other, unlike the first time we met, but we did do a lot of talking and walking. I remember walking from Grimsby to Cleethorpes, where we had tea, then back to Grimsby. She insisted on paying for her own tea, she said "I don't know you well enough yet to let you pay for me". We got on splendidly together. I'm sure we told each other the history of our lives and made arrangements to meet again the following Sunday, again with the request that I come in uniform.

On my next visit Edna took me to her home to meet her family, her father, her brother and her step-sister who kept home for them. Her mother had died and her step-sister was a widow. I was given a wonderful welcome and asked what seemed like hundreds of questions especially by her brother who intended to join the RAF when old enough. I made several visits after that before I was posted away from Manby, sometimes selling the 1/- books of postage stamps that had been sent to me from relations to get money to pay the bus fare to Grimsby. Edna did come to Louth to see me one Sunday, but Louth was dead from Saturday night until Monday morning and there was nowhere to go, so we didn't repeat the experience.

In June we had what was then known as Empire Air Day. This was the day when selected RAF stations were open to the public, Manby being one of the open stations. I believe the entrance fee was 2/6d and like the air shows of today there was a flying display and a static display of aircraft. At that open day we also had two ground floor rooms of a barrack block prepared as for a Saturday morning inspection and open for the public to view, ours being the nearest barrack block to the hangars it fell to us to exhibit the Bull.

Every one of us had a duty of some kind to perform on the day, even if it was only to walk around the camp in best blue and look busy but be observant. My duty for the day was to enquire of the visitors, when they purchased their entrance tickets, if they had a camera and if this was so to take possession of the camera for the duration of the show, giving a receipt of course. I don't remember collecting many cameras, most people I suppose kept them in their pockets and who was I to doubt their words. Besides, with the antiquated lot of aircraft we had at Manby we had no secret weapons that any foreign powers might want to get hold of, and the only aircraft of the interesting kind that had been flown in for the day were roped off and a good distance from the spectators.

Our exams were approaching now and this meant that I did a lot of extra swotting. Bomb sights were still an enigma to me but I was confident I was well versed in all the other subjects. We did have a few members of the course who were brilliant, but the remainder were like myself, just happy to know we had a chance of passing the exam.

I still made my visits to the tarmac whenever possible on a Saturday morning and I really enjoyed the flights, long or short, sometimes in Fairey Gordons or Westland Wallaces but mostly in Hawker Harts or Hinds. It was about this time that one of the drogue towing aircraft crashed into the sea, the drogue cable having become tangled in the tail of the aircraft, the pilot and the drogue operator being killed. This led me to see for the first time a deceased airman's kit being auctioned in the Dining Hall the next day, the proceeds being for the next of kin. This was the accepted custom in the RAF.

The starting day for our exams was to be Monday, July 10th. A little panic now, was I good enough? How was I in this or that subject? Questions about this and answers about that amongst each other in our room. Then the day dawned and for a whole week it was the forward and backward movements of breech blocks and why; the components of this and that; firing pins feed mechanisms, solenoids; magazines.

Why is it called bomb pistol? How does a bob fuse function? What is amatol? What is baratol? What is cordite used for? Dismantle this gun, assemble that gun, how does synchronising gear work? In gun sighting what is deflection? How does wind speed or airspeed affect a falling bomb? Questions and questions. They weren't so difficult, it was describing the actions of this and that on paper that proved the hardest.

Then exam results, and our new ranks as Armourers, Trade Group 2, and our postings. These were given on July 18th. We had one lad who had a 90 plus pass who was upgraded to Leading Aircraftmen and I think about 12 lads who were upgraded to Aircraftmen Cass 1, and the remainder of us were re-classified as Aircraftmen Class 2 Armourers, the promotions to take effect from July 19th, 1939.

Flight Sergeant Fisher was, to say the least, jumping over the moon. His first course and no failures! All 65 of us had passed and even the lowest marks among us were well up about the 60% mark. This meant that my pay immediately rose from 14/- to, I think, 28/- per week and all found, this all happening in the short time since the previous October when I was slaving for 18/3d per week in the tinplate industry.

Where was I posted to? There was pushing and shoving to see the list on the notice board. Who was going with whom? Where was this place? Where is Birchham Newton? Where is Feltwell? One was posted to No 41 Squadron, another to No 56 Squadron. We were being scattered far and wide. My posting was to No 19 (Fighter) Squadron at Duxford and my companion was to be Jimmy Belton. He was from the next room and all the course were to move on Friday, July 21st. John Andrews, my close friend, was posted to a fighter squadron somewhere in the south-east, I have forgotten where. We went to bomber squadrons, fighter squadrons and Coastal Command squadrons all over the country.

There wasn't time to see Edna before my move. I knew she would be as disappointed as I was. I had applied for a posting to North Coates which was a Coastal Command station near Cleethorpes, but I don't remember anyone going to the station of their choice.

Our last day in Manby, and a surprise for Flight Sergeant Fisher and his good lady wife. They were invited to our barrack block in the afternoon and there the Flight was presented with an inscribed pocket watch from the whole course as a token our great esteem for him, with a promise from him that there would be no more illicit borrowing of watches from bomb sight cases! Mrs Fisher was presented with a picnic basket for allowing us to take up so much of her husband's time in the previous months. The money had been donated by all members of our course, who had given what they could afford over the previous four weeks.

Then a celebration evening in the village pub at Grimoldby crossroads, the same pub that showed us its friendly lights that first cold, wet and miserable night we arrived at Manby so long ago in January.

Chapter Six

DUXFORD

I got off the train at Peterborough, the lads throwing my kit and hat after me with a lot of good riddance and ribbing. I wondered whether I would ever see any of them again. I had said my goodbyes to the lads going North and West at Manby, and Flight Sergeant Fisher had given all of us his good wishes and a handshake at Grimoldby station.

There I was standing on the platform of Peterborough station, but where was Jimmy Belton? I looked all along the platform but there was no airman in sight. Jim had been travelling with his mates in another coach. I checked my Movement Order, yes, change at Peterborough and March. I though Jim had missed the stop and would get off at the next station and return. Time for a cup of tea in the buffet, and the sandwiches supplied by the kitchen staff at Manby, but afterwards still no Jim. So off I went across the town to the Peterborough East Railway Station and the train to March. When I arrived at March there was Jim sat on a seat on the platform waiting for the Cambridge train. He had been waiting there an hour; unbeknown to me he had been routed to travel changing trains at Spalding and March, and had therefore travelled with some of the lads going to bomber stations in Norfolk.

Whittlesford at last. This was the railway station for Duxford. I remember Jim saying, "We are in luck, there is a RAF truck outside the station, perhaps we can get a lift", but the truck driver told us this was a normal duty on Fridays (RAF Postings day) to meet the trains, besides we were expected so it was no coincidence. He also told us it was about one and-a-half miles to the camp.

We were soon at the Guard Room and No 19 Squadron's Armoury was pointed out to us about fifty yards away. One of the RAF Police was immediately despatched there to tell of our arrival. An N.C.O came across to us and announced himself as Corporal Marchant. He told us he was in charge of the Squadron Armoury, along with Sergeant Ranner, and he was our Junior N.C.O. Asking us to accompany him, he took us across the Newmarket to Royston road (which ran through the centre of the camp) to the domestic area and to the Squadron Barrack block. He also told us we had joined a fighter squadron and that ours was the first squadron in the RAF to have Spitfires, which replaced Gloster Gauntlets in August 1938.

We had an apology from the Corporal because armourers' room was already over-crowded with extra beds around the walls, and in some cases two sharing a locker. Jim and I were allocated beds in the centre of the room, one each end of the table with a wooden chest each for our kit pushed under the bed. Most of the beds were occupied by motor drivers and airmen (general duties). We were only eight armourers, including Corporal Marchant, in the room. The ninth armourer, A/C Stanley, was married and lived in Duxford village. We were told to settle ourselves in and assured that our room mates-to-be would look after us when they came off duty.

Full of enthusiasm and expecting to see aircraft everywhere, Jim and I were surprised to be told that the Squadron was always quiet and partly shut for the weekend. Of course, this was the 'Strawberry and Cream and Fruitcake for Tea' period of Air Force history, when half the Squadron staff went on weekend leave each weekend.

We were to learn that a little flying was done by No 19 Squadron and by No 66 Squadron, our fellow squadron, on Saturday mornings. Most of the weekend flying was done by Cambridge University Air Squadron with their Avro Tutors. We were also to learn from the other armourers that evening that the Squadron Armoury Staff, including Jim and myself, were: -

Sergeant Ranner	Fitter Armourer
Corporal Marchant	Fitter Armourer
A/C Stanley	Armourer
A/C Plunket	Armourer}Eastchurch
A/C O'Brennan	Armourer}trained
A/C Owen	Armourer}Halton trained
A/C Pickles	Armourer
A/C Clayton	Armourer} Manby
A/C Roberts	Armourer} trained
A/C Belton	Armourer}

We all came under the jurisdiction of the Squadron Engineering Officer and the Station Armament Officer.

After parade the next morning we were marched to the Armoury, Corporal Marchant being in charge and upon arrival we were introduced to Sergeant Ranner who made us welcome and allocated me to "A" Flight and Jim to "B". He also told us to walk around the hangar with the lads and familiarise ourselves with the Spitfire. Even today I still remember the thrill, the first time I sat in the cockpit of that Spitfire and had the control column in my hand. Of all the hundreds of times I sat in Spitfires in later years, it was never like that first time. Another thing that greeted us in the Armoury was the clothes line, complete with feminine underwear, brassieres, knickers, etc. These we were told were the spoils of war. No sexual victories were to be boasted about unless accompanied with a trophy, but we found later in the morning that the trophies were really salvaged from the rags issued from the stores for gun cleaning and were hung as decorations in an otherwise dreary room. We also had to report to all the various offices in Station Headquarters, such as Station Orderly Room and Accounts, and get ourselves pass-out cards, then to the Squadron Orderly Room where we were told to report again on the following Monday morning to see the Squadron Adjutant.

Saturday afternoons were free, there were no compulsory Church Parades on Sundays or any other weekend duties, and no guard or fire picket duties. The guard duties were carried out by the RAF Police.

The Station C.O was Wing Commander Woodhall, who would later command great fame and respect as Sector Controller at Duxford and Tangmere during the Battle of Britain and afterwards. No 19 Squadron was commanded by Squadron Leader Cozens AFC.

Very little happened at Duxford during the period between my arrival and September 3rd, 1939. It was Parade on the Square to 0800 hrs Monday to Friday, for morning prayers and colour raising and march to the hangars. If weather permitted flying it was 2-6 on the hangar doors, wheel out the aircraft, then daily inspections outside, sign Form 700 and then mostly local flying until 1600 hrs, Spitfires back in the hangar, 2-6 to close the doors and march back to the Barrack Block. There was talk at this time of the Squadron going to RAF Sutton Bridge, a bombing and gunnery range near Kings Lynn, in September. This was to be the Squadron's annual Air to Air and Air to Ground firing exercises and there was a period of a few nights early in August when I recall the Squadron participating in some Home Defence exercises with the Anti-Aircraft and Searchlight units in Cambridgeshire, but I didn't take part in this. Armourers were not needed, other than to carry out their daily aircraft inspections.

I must make mention of the tool kit I was issued with. This consisted of a wooden box 18 inches square and 10 inches deep (lockable if one had some keys), a pair of six inch pliers, an eight inch screwdriver, an oil can and two B A spanner, full stop. Despite the claims of lots of people that we used our Field Service caps to cock the Browning Guns, I never heard of this or saw it happen. We would have had to buy a new cap if we had damaged ours in any way. We all had a cocking toggle that we made with a piece of thick fence wire and a three inch piece of broom handle. This we were never without when on duty. Another invaluable tool was a round of .303 ball or armour piercing ammunition. The point of the bullet was the best tool to remove and replace the breech block return spring of a Browning gun.

Charlie Stanley (Stan) who first introduced me to Spitfires had sort of taken me under his wing and we became great friends. We became a team, working together and thus making our daily inspection and other maintenance work easier. Stan had been with the Squadron when 19 had Gloster Gauntlets, and so had been working on Spits from the start so he was well able to pass on vast experience. There was so much new that I learned from him. For a start there was the jargon. Anything that flew was a kite, not a Spit or a Hurricane or a Wellington, and when the word 'DOORS' was shouted by 'A' or 'B' Flight Chiefy, one didn't look around to see where it was, everyone within hearing immediately found somewhere to hide, in a cockpit, under benches, behind trestles, anywhere, as the call meant hard work pushing open or closing the hangar doors, no easy job on the old Duxford hangar doors! '2-6' was the shout to push when sufficient bodies had been conscripted to do the job, and also the call to lift, when lifting an aircraft onto trestles, or any physical work requiring more than two of us.

There were the aircraft to be pushed in and out of the hangar daily, the Daily Inspections to be carried out and the Forms 700 (serviceability forms) to be signed. I was expected to assist the Flight Mechanics Engine and Airframe to start up the aircraft by connecting up the accumulator starter trolley, pressing the button on the signal from the cockpit and disconnecting the cable from the engine after starting, taking care not to walk into the spinning propeller while doing so. I was also expected to lend my body weight to the tail plane while the Flight Mechanic or pilot revved up the engine and blew my head off, or so it seemed. As part of the team on a particular aircraft I also assisted in steadying the aircraft while it was being taxied over the grass area by holding the wing tip. There were also times when I was required to pull the wheel chocks away on the pilot's request. These were all duties we were never taught at Armament School.

Then there was still the "Bull" that I had encountered at Uxbridge and Manby, such as floor polishing and the lining up of lockers and beds and general cleanliness of the room, but as tradesmen we didn't have the ablution chores as previous. These were done by general duty airmen and there wasn't the rigorous discipline I had previously known.

Cambridge University Air Squadron left Duxford on August 13th, and were re-located at Marshall's Flying Training School (FTS) at Cambridge. They were replaced by No 611 'County of West Lancashire' Auxiliary Squadron, which took over the vacant hangar. They also flew Spitfires and our ground crews soon developed the same friendly rivalry with our auxiliary colleagues as we had with No 66 Squadron, our companion regular RAF Squadron at Duxford.

I knew I had some leave due to me, not having had any since Easter of that year, and I had been saving my money so that I could spend the leave visiting Edna at Grimsby. I had written to her telling her of my plans and we were both looking forward to my impending visit, when on the August 24th, all leave was stopped and those personnel on leave were recalled. We all knew there was a possibility of war being declared against Germany, but none of us at thought it was really so serious. How was I to explain in a letter to Edna that all our plans were to no avail and it was likely that months might elapse before we were to see each other again? As things turned out, the events of the next few weeks did all the explaining for me.

It was also at this time that all the Living Out Permits were cancelled for the married personnel so it meant Charlie Stanley, our colleague, having to come back into the Barrack Room to reside. Fortunately this coincided with most of the Motor Transport Drivers and Aircraftmen G/Ds in our room being posted to France, so there were beds for all. Once again I had a bed against the wall and a steel locker. I settled for a bed next to Stan. The Married Quarters were also vacated at this time and shortly afterwards began to be filled with WAAFs (female personnel of the Women's Auxiliary Air Force).

I spent many an evening in the 'Air-o-Drome Café' with my fellow armourers. This café was on the Newmarket Road, just beyond the Officers' Mess and towards Whittlesford Station. We usually called there after booking in at the Guard Room on returning from Cambridge, or we took a stroll there after the NAAFI closed at 2130 hrs. Everyone's favourite was tea and Lyons individual fruit pies, which I believe were 4d each and a mug (usually chipped) of tea cost 2d. Did the Café have an old biplane on the roof? I can't remember, but I do remember the wonderful collection of old wooden propellers that were arranged around the walls inside. What happened to them all when the Café was demolished, I wonder?

Another pre-war activity was swimming on a Sunday morning in Whittlesford Mill pond, daring the wrath of the local bobby "Whittlesford Willie". It was said he made a clean sweep one Sunday, gathering up and temporarily confiscating several sets of uniforms, but that was before my time.

Working on the aircraft I found that the pilots were just ordinary people and often the pilot of a plane I was working on would have a chat about the plane or the armament, and perhaps even make some suggestion. The N.C.O pilots I found were the best, perhaps because they had come through the ranks, and most of the commissioned officers were also easy to talk to. Jimmy Belton and I were taken and introduced to the Squadron Adjutant, Pilot Officer Brinsden, on the Monday following our arrival at Duxford and he immediately put us at ease. Our 'A' Flight Commander, Flight Lieutenant Withall, sometimes came and had a chat, but we saw little of the C.O, Squadron Leader Cozens.

Sergeant Ranner left us at this time, the end of August 1939, to attend a Senior N.C.Os' Armament Course at Manby. This left Corporal (Tommy) Marchant in charge of the Squadron Armoury.

Chapter Seven

Arming for War

We had a number of Volunteer Reserve (VR) airmen posted to us in the first few days of September. They had been called up under the Mobilisation Order of August 29th and were mostly local people. I remember that two were from Haverhill, and one from Newmarket, but another was a lad from a Barnardo home. They all had some knowledge of machine-guns and were classed as Armourers' Assistants. I think the two from Haverhill did their training at RAF Debden. We also had a Class 'E' Reservist, Corporal Lowe, posted to us. He had been in the Royal Flying Corps and his talk was of Sopwith Camels, Spads and SE5s, Vickers and Lewis machine-guns. He was immediately given work in the Armoury Office.

September 2nd, and immediately after I had carried out my Daily Inspection and signed the Form 700, three other of our armament staff and I were all sent along with some of No 66 Squadron's personnel, with a couple of lorries and drivers, to Whittlesford Railway Station. There we found seven or eight rail wagons, all full of .303 ammunition waiting to be unloaded and transported to the ammunition dump at Duxford. This meant at least two or perhaps three days work. I can still see the trains travelling through the station, passing us at frequent intervals, full of evacuee children and their school teachers, all from London and all travelling to Norfolk, waving madly.

Sunday, September 3ʳᵈ, 1939; after Daily Inspection, back to the railway station again to carry on with the unloading. More evacuee trains passing through, then at 1100 hrs, the landlord of the 'Railway Tavern', adjacent to the goods yard, invited us all into his back room and drew us all a pint of his best ale, *gratis*. He switched on his radio and we listened together to Chamberlain's speech declaring 'war' on Germany. The landlord had taken us into his back room because he wasn't allowed to have us in the bar, it not being 12 noon.

Shortly after the declaration of war, the local air raid sirens were screaming and from the station yard we saw No 19 and No 66 Squadron aircraft take off and circle around before landing again. I remember one of the lads saying at the time, "I don't know what good they can do except ram any Germans, there's no ammo in them Spitfires we have got it all here!"

The transporting of the ammo now complete, I was again one of a party for a couple of days making up the ammo into belts of 300 rounds each. We were allocated a room next to the Main Stores for this purpose. I can't remember the order in which the belts were made at this time, but I know they contained ball, armour piercing, incendiary and tracer. A mystery occurred at this time. We had a young ex-apprentice armourer working with us and he chalked slogans outside and inside our little ammo room, all in German; then, after a few days, he disappeared with no word or explanation to anyone. We never saw him again.

Back to the Squadron full time now and all of us armourers and assistants were practising re-arming for hours every day until two armourers and two assistants could change all of a Spitfire's eight ammo tanks, cock all the guns and replace all the panels in around three minutes flat.

While we carried out our activities, the Flight Mech's Airframe were re-spraying the Spitfires with war camouflage and changing the Squadron identity letters from W Z to Q V. While the Flight Mech's Engine were helping Rolls Royce personnel to change the two-bladed Watt's propeller to three-bladed De Havilland variable pitch propellers, plus other modifications, we were removing the camera guns from the starboard wing stub and installing cine cameras inside the port wing stub. Some of the Spitfires were also still fitted with ring and bead sights, which had to be replaced with reflector sights.

About this time we were all detailed in groups to attend the Clothing Store where we handed in our ceremonial peaked hats (only commissioned officers, warrant officers and RAF Police were to wear peaked hats in the future), and we were all issued with a waterproof groundsheet/cape and a steel helmet. Those personnel working on the airfield were also issued with a pair of Wellington boots.

The beginning of September also saw Flight Lieutenant Withall, the 'A' Flight Commander, leave us, and he was replaced by Flight Lieutenant Brian Lane, who came from No 213 Hurricane Squadron. He became our new 'A' Flight Commander.

Our Squadron was now flying to RAF Watton in Norfolk on a flight basis, changing daily with No 66 Squadron and were doing North Sea patrols, guarding shipping. We also dispersed the planes every day to the boundary of Duxford airfield, bringing them back into the hangars every night.

We had a mobile office and Pilots' Room at the dispersal, and a large marquee which we used as a workshop and shelter when the weather was of an adverse nature. Our dispersal was at the Royston side of Duxford airfield. At this time, contractors started constructing taxiing strips, hard standings, and parking bays around the airfield and I can recall us all rabbit hunting when the bulldozers tore up the hedgerows, the rabbits being taken home by the lads who lived locally.

One day in September, I was detailed by Corporal Marchant to travel with him by road to the BSA Factory at Small Heath, Birmingham, to fetch several hundred of the new Mk of Browning guns for No 19 and No 66 Squadrons. These guns had no flash eliminator, but had a new type of muzzle choke which gave them a faster rate of fire and made for less fouling in the choke than the old flash eliminator. This made maintenance easier and gave longer life to the barrel. It also meant that now the gun ports could be covered, whereas before the flash eliminators of the two outer guns, port and starboard side protruded forward of the leading edges of the wings, thus preventing this.

On our trip to Birmingham we stopped for breakfast at a transport café at Weedon, and there tried our luck on the one-armed bandit on a share-all basis with the lorry driver. Only two sixpences were necessary. Our lucky day, we hit the jackpot of over £12, a lot of money to us. We had our midday meal in the canteen at the BSA factory and whilst waiting for the guns to be loaded, we explored and found a warehouse with hundreds of bicycles all destined for the RAF. We tried hard but no amount of persuading could get us even one, and we tried for three, on each, but the AID Inspector in charge of them was a hard man. Anyway we did manage to sort out the guns and mark the boxes. All those carrying heavily greased guns we marked up for No 66 Squadron, and those that were ungreased (in the majority) were to be allocated to No 19 Squadron, as per our quota, and the rest to No 66 Squadron.

These guns meant a lot of hard work for us all in the Squadron Armoury. For the next few weeks there was the stripping and thorough cleaning of the guns to be done, the feeds had to be altered on a lot of the guns as 50% had to be left-hand feed and 50% right-hand feed. Then the old guns had to be removed from the Spitfires and the new guns installed, the aircraft taken to the firing butts and their new guns harmonised with the reflector sight, the installation and harmonisation then being checked by the pilot. The eight guns were then lock-nutted and wired, then test-fired. I spent days and days on my knees under the wings doing this work. We had to push the Spitfires to the butts and manually lift them onto the trestles for levelling before harmonising, all hard work.

There were a couple of occasions when we had to return to work in the evening to finish the gun changing and harmonising because that aircraft was required the next morning. At this time part of our hangar was being used in the evening by the WAAFs, who were being taught drill procedures. Of course, there had to be the occasional wolf whistle from some of the lads while the girls were marching away from the Sergeant WAAF in Charge, but did we get a right ear full the times she heard. She was a right battleaxe and her language could be stronger than ours!

We hardly had time to notice that a new Squadron, No 222 (F), was being formed at Duxford. We were so tired at the day's end that we never bothered to go further than the Air-O-Drome Café or the NAAFI, and perhaps a Sunday night stroll to one of the pubs in Whittlesford. There was a card school going every night in the Barrack Room (illegally), the games being Rummy or Pontoon, the stakes never more than 2d. I never gambled. I still had my sights set on that leave in Grimsby, whenever it might be. Edna and I still corresponded.

On October 6th, whilst returning from Watton, Flying Officer Ball flew into Flight Lieutenant Clouston, damaging the tail of the latter's Spitfire. He made an emergency landing at Newmarket racecourse. Neither of the pilots was injured. I didn't see anything of the aircraft, they both being from 'B' Flight. No 611 Squadron left Duxford on October 10th, flying to their new base at Digby in Lincolnshire.

We Armourers and assistants of 'A' Flight were given two hours to pack our kit on October 19th. We had heard rumours of an impending move to Scotland, but were told to report to the Guard Room for transport to Cambridge Railway Station. We were going to RAF Catterick in Yorkshire by train, the rest of 'A' Flight personnel flying the following day.

I had better mention one of our Armourers who joined us in September, as his name will keep coming up from time to time in my story; forgetting his name, I will call him John. I remember his parents kept the 'Angel' pub in Islington, London. If there were any clangers to be dropped, John dropped them. On our journey to Catterick we had a two hour wait at Peterborough. John went off lady-killing while the rest of us sought a meal in the Sally-Ann (Salvation Army canteen), near the railway station. He came back with seconds to spare and caught the train. Halfway to Doncaster, John remembered that he had left his kitbag on the platform at Peterborough! Fortunately he had it forwarded to Catterick a few days later.

I was walking along the tarmac at Catterick on the second morning after our arrival when I heard a loud voice with a broad Scottish accent calling "Fred!" It was none other than Sandy Stuart, my first friend from our Uxbridge days. He was now an Electrician on No 41 Squadron, which we had replaced at Catterick. They had moved temporarily to RAF Drem at Edinburgh, but Sandy, being in Maintenance Flight, had remained behind. We then enjoyed a few evenings relating our experiences and talking of our days at Uxbridge.

We had a few occasions whilst at Catterick when one or other of the sections were vectored after enemy aircraft but never saw a thing. On one occasion, however, a section met up with the enemy but were prevented from engaging by Anti-Aircraft fire put up by the Royal Navy. There was one exciting incident when one of our Spits came roaring back on his own from a patrol, leaking glycol like a vapour trail. Everyone thought he had been hit by enemy return fire, but I cannot remember if this was so. We returned to Duxford on October 27th, the whole of our ground personnel flying back in two stripped out Imperial Airways Ensigns. We landed at Duxford after dark and I think the whole of the station personnel were on the tarmac to greet us. Our journey back, although a bit bumpy, was a lot better than the train journey North!

No 222 Squadron had the first of their aircraft arrive on November 1st. These were Mk 1 short-nosed Blenheims, armed with four Browning guns in a pod under the nose and one Vickers K gun in the Bristol turret in the rear. This Squadron took over the hangar vacated by No 611 Squadron. Our Squadron and No 66 Squadron were now flying to a new RAF station at Horsham St Faith on the outskirts of Norwich, instead of Watton, but were still patrolling the shipping on the North Sea as previously.

It was in November that a detachment of about 20 Flight Mechs Engine, Airframe and Armourers, a Cook and a Motor Driver were sent to St Faith's as a refuelling and re-arming unit. The personnel were to be changed every two weeks. I was made part of this unit late in November, replacing Maurice-Owen. We were all billeted in a private house named 'Red Roofs', that had been commandeered and the residents moved elsewhere, when the airfield construction commenced. This house was situated in Fifers Lane on the city side boundary of the airfield. We had a mobile field kitchen at the back of the house and were totally self-contained, rations being sent weekly from Duxford by road, mail being sent daily in the flare tube of the Flight Leader's Spitfire.

'A' Flight or 'B' Flight, and sometimes both flights, flew to St Faith's daily, alternating with No 66 Squadron, weather permitting, and remained at St Faith's flying from there as and when required until dusk when they returned to Duxford.

While on the ground at St Faith's the aircraft were dispersed close to the boundary fence in Fifers Lane. At weekends we had hundreds of Norwich people lined up along the fence waiting for things to happen. Sometimes the pilots gave them a miniature air display before flying off back to Duxford around 1530 – 1600 hrs. The front room of the house was the pilots' rest room during the daytime. Also in the ground floor back there was a radio transmitting and receiving station, and the telephone in there was manned 24 hours a day. We had a wooden building of the type normally used for accommodation in the back garden but this was unusable other than for rough storage. It had no heating or lighting and it was overrun with rats. The novelty of the detachment and being free of restrictions soon wore off with 20 or so airmen sharing the three bedrooms and sleeping four inches off the floor on bedboards that didn't make for comfort. There was only one toilet and bathroom between us and then besides having to help prepare all our food we had to sit on the bedboards with our plates on our knees to eat it. There was also the question of laundry. We had to do our own.

I had notification the first week in December that I had been promoted to A/C 1 Armourer. I can't remember how much this meant in cash value but it was welcome. I wasn't alone in all this as all the tradesmen were upgraded, the A/C1s being promoted to Leading Aircraftmen.

After the Spits returned to Duxford the time was our own. We had no booking out or restrictions of any kind but we stayed in the house most nights. We spent an occasional Wednesday evening and every Saturday evening at the Norwich Lido Ballroom (entry fee 6d). It was mostly a drink and a chat in the warmth of the Dance Hall as only a few of the lads could dance. I never learned. I should have returned to Duxford before Christmas but for some unknown reason none of the Armament staff were changed and we were left at Norwich where we spent the whole of the festive season and into January at 'Red Roofs'. We all had a good Christmas aiding the Cook with the preparation of all the meals. We were also invited to a few local homes on Boxing Day.

It was soon after Christmas that we had a lot of snow when the roads in Norfolk were blocked and we were unable to obtain rations from Duxford, but we had rations supplied to us from RAF Watton when they sent supplies to a detachment of No 21 Bomber Squadron, which was on the Old Catton side of St Faith's airfield. There was a telephone instruction at this time from the Station Armament Officer at Duxford informing the Armourers that the belts of re-arms of ammunition we held were to be immediately broken down and re-made as per four ball, two armour piercing, one incendiary, one tracer, this repeated. But first we had to dig out the ammunition. The ammo bunker was under three feet of snow. I think there were about twenty re-arms, that was one hundred and sixty belts to be altered, that was forty-eight thousand rounds to be handled. We had to do this in the unheated wooden hut. It was a long and cold job which we finished by candlelight, which one of us had to go out and buy. The Corporal in charge of the detachment insisted that there was to be no finishing the job tomorrow and we had no assistance from the other tradesmen.

We were informed that from January 1ˢᵗ, 1940, Squadron Leader Cozens would be leaving the Squadron on being promoted to Wing Commander. Our new Squadron Commanding Officer would be Squadron Leader Stephenson, who had been a Chief Flying Instructor (CFI) at the Central Flying School (CFS).

On January 11th, three of No 66 Squadron Spitfires took off from St Faith's on a normal North Sea patrol but were vectored onto a Heinkel 111, which they disabled (later we were to learn that it crashed in Denmark), but one of the Spitfires had to make a wheels-up forced landing on the cliff tops somewhere near Cromer. My colleagues and I went out there to unload the guns. We couldn't take out the ammo tanks because of the wings being on the ground so we had to stay and guard the plane until it was removed much later that day.

I returned to Duxford in late January and was fortunate to take up my old bed and locker next to Charlie Stanley.

In so short a time a lot had happened at the station. 'A' and 'B' Flights were now permanently based on the airfield boundary but we still had the same mobile office and marquee workshop in which to work and shelter. There were also some new faces in the Armoury. Corporal Lowe had been posted so we were back to just Tommy Marchant in charge. For me it was back to daily inspections and all the other routine maintenance work associated with the aircraft.

There was heavy snow that first week in February and it was freezing cold, colder even than it had been at Norwich a month earlier. For days flying was impossible.

I was walking across the hangar from the armoury to the ground crew rest room on February 8th when I saw this new pilot, a flying officer, in front of me walking with a queer lurching gait. I asked questions in the rest room and was told it was Flying Officer Douglas Bader who had lost both legs in a flying accident in December 1931; he now walked on two metal legs. We were all wondering what position he was going to hold on the Squadron, not realising that he intended to fly as part of the Squadron's complement of pilots. A little later that day he gave us a magnificent display of aerobatics in the Squadron Miles Magister. We were also to learn that he was a great friend of Squadron Leader Stephenson, with whom he formed part of an aerobatic team in 1931.

Perhaps it was a bonus for my long spell at Norwich, but I was granted a Weekend Pass in the middle of February, this being from after duty on Friday until 2359 hrs on Sunday. This too was a 20th Birthday present, being close to the 17th of the month. I was off to Grimsby at last! I had plenty of time to inform Edna but had no idea of the time of the trains and so could give no arrival times. What a journey! I got to Peterborough 2220 hrs but the last train to Grimsby for the day had left at 2210 hrs. There were about 12 of us stranded, all servicemen, mostly RAF and RN. 'No!', we were told we had not missed a booked connection, it was a normal service and we could not stop the night at the station. The next train to Grimsby was 0600 hrs on Saturday morning and it was normal for service people to spend the night in the Salvation Army Canteen near the station.

I've never stopped thanking the Salvation Army for their kindness to the Armed Forces during the war, not just for their looking after us when they gave us food and warmth and shelter for less than 2/-, but for all the many occasions they showed their presence when other organisations were prominent by absence only. But more of that later.

I arrived at Thomas Street where Edna lived about 0900 hrs, tired, dirty and hungry. I will always remember the welcome I received from Doris, Edna's stepsister. It was like going home. I was given Edna's brother's bedroom. He had joined the RAF since the war started. A hot bath was soon ready and a good meal followed, then there were all the questions asked by both Doris and Edna's father. I wasn't to see Edna until noon when she finished work, then I had the fuss all over again. It seemed hours before we were left to ourselves, then there was so much to talk about. All those things young couples have to say to each other. The time flew by. I had to catch an early train on the Sunday morning. The war was already affecting the railway service limiting the number of trains. I know it was a sad farewell on Grimsby Station with a promise that I would be back as soon as possible.

I had to change trains at Spalding and there met (Clappy) Clayton, my fellow 19 Squadron Armourer who was also returning from a 48 hour pass, we had about four hours to wait for the next train. We wandered around the town and had a meal in a canteen run by the Women's Voluntary Service

(WVS) in a building in the cattle marker near the railway station. We arrived back at Whittlesford early in the evening. It was an evening soon after my weekend off that John, our 'Jonah', came into the Barrack Room plastered with mud, his overcoat and trousers were thick with it and he was soaking wet. Also he had lost his cap. He had taken a WAAF for a walk around the airfield, in the dark of course, but the fools had got into a slit trench for perhaps you know what. It had been raining hard that day and the walls of the trench crumbled with their bumping against them and the sides caved in on them. Luckily they were able to scramble out. I would have like to know if the 'Queen WAAF' found out and if so, what was said. John was lucky, he heard nothing of the incident other than our leg pulling.

I was detailed on February 29th to go with others to Whittlesford, where Spitfire K9809 had dived into the ground the previous night whilst practising night time take-offs and landings. The pilot, Pilot Officer Trenchard, was killed. I was horrified when I got there. The place was in small pieces, the engine everywhere; one belt of ammo was wrapped around an oleo leg, the wheel of which was 400 yards away. I had the propeller tip from this aircraft made into a picture frame. The second tip was taken by Charlie Stanley, the third was too badly damaged to be of any use. We salvaged the propeller tips from the Duxford aircraft graveyard a few days after the crash.

No 222 Squadron started changing their Blenheims for Spitfires at this time and we lost some of our Squadron personnel, of all trades, to them, both Tommy Plunket and Maurice Owen going from the Armament Section.

I returned to Horsham St Faith around the middle of March, this time taking John with me. We replaced two Armourers who returned to Duxford. Nothing had changed there since I had left in January, the conditions were exactly the same but the weather had improved and we had more daylight hours. We also had the aircraft coming in daily. On March 23rd, one section of 'A' Flight was taking off from Horsham, led by Flying Officer Bader. We were watching, but what has happening? Bader didn't seem to be rising to any height. One of the Flight Mechs with us shouted, "The silly bugger's in coarse pitch.", and that is what it proved to be. The Spitfire hit the stone wall bounding the airfield and made a belly landing on the other side. Today it would be classified as pilot error, but then it was a bloody great gaffe. In the pile-up Bader bent his metal legs badly. It could have been worse had he not had those legs!

We still had those flights every day patrolling over the shipping on the North Sea. The aircraft returned to Duxford every evening until April 17th, when the whole of 'A' and 'B' Flights moved to St Faith's on a semi-permanent basis. We were kicked out of our 'Red Roofs' and for the first couple of nights slept on the floor of one of the new hangars. After that we were moved to an old army barracks that had been used by No 21 Squadron, their availability state still being on the wall, complete with the last entries.

Upon the Squadron's arrival the new Dining Hall and cook-house was opened. This made conditions so much better for us. 'Red Roofs' was now being used by the pilots and administration staff.

A section of 'B' Flight, consisting of Flight Lieutenant Clouston, Flying Officer Petre and Flight Sergeant Steere, were on patrol on May 11th when they encountered a Junkers 88 which they shot down in the sea. This was No 19 Squadron's first victory. It was soon after this, on May 16th, that we all moved back to Duxford.

Chapter Eight

DUXFORD & HORNCHURCH

The Balloon Goes Up!

Back at Duxford I soon settled into the old routine of marching to work after the Morning Parade on the Square, unless I was rostered for an early morning duty at the Dispersal or if I had been on night duty. We had quite a large body of men in the Section by this time and were detailed to carry out Daily Inspections on any one or even two of the Spitfires.

I was to become the Armourer to Flight Sergeant George Unwin and be responsible for the armament on Spitfire QV-H for 'Harry'. There were also numerous occasions when I did the maintenance on other Spitfires as well as on my own aircraft, such as when the other armourers were on leave etc, and I was always to work as a team with Stan, whose aircraft was QV-K. During a re-arming session all armourers were expected to join in.

We weren't to stay at Duxford very long. May 25th saw us move to RAF Hornchurch in Essex. The 'balloon had gone up'. French, British and Belgian Forces in France were in full retreat from the Germans and so the Squadron was to help cover the retreating forces at Calais and Dunkirk. We made the journey to Hornchurch by road, the pilots flying the Spitfires there the same evening.

A little story again about John. During our short stay at Duxford, John had been granted a 48 hour pass to go home to Islington. There his dad had bought him an AJS motorbike. On his return on it to camp the bike broke down about one and-a-half miles from the airfield. He left the bike in a field and walked to camp. Next morning, with the assistance of a couple of his mates, the bike was pushed to the dispersal via the hedge and boundary fence (not having permission for the bike he couldn't enter via the Guard Room). On examination after striping the bike and engine, Paddy O'Brennan, our Irish motor bike expert, pronounced the engine seized because there was no oil left in the sump. Anyway next came the announcement, pack up everything, the Squadron is going to Hornchurch. What was John to do with the bike all in pieces? They could be taken with us and John was insistent that no one else should have it, so the bike finished up being dumped down a well in some old farm buildings beyond the boundary, Duxford village side of the airfield, money down the drain, or should I say well!

Next morning, May 26th, it was 0500 hrs at Dispersal and Daily Inspections in the dark, which was to be our norm for the next couple of weeks. It was very early when the Squadron took off that first morning but Flight Sergeant Unwin was unlucky. There were 14 pilots, two having come by road but only 12 Spitfires, and he lost the draw for places. I can't remember who flew QV-H in his place, but on returning I could see that all the guns had been fired (because the patches covering the gun ports had all been blown away). It was a quick re-arm, but as the planes returned, mostly individually it was a case of all mucking in on a single aircraft, a quick clean out of the gun barrels, a drop of oil on the breech block and once again, ready.

What price all the teaching we had at Manby? After every firing of the guns, the barrel must be removed and boiled in caustic soda to remove the fouling, the breech block stripped and thoroughly cleaned and oiled, etc, etc, and the number of rounds fired entered in the gun log book. Where could we boil guns on the far side of Hornchurch airfield? I shudder to think what George Unwin would have said if I told him he couldn't have his aircraft during a 'flap' because I was boiling his guns, and the last time I had seen a log book was when we took the guns out of the boxes after bringing them from BSA!

Sadly during that first encounter with the *Luftwaffe*, we lost our C.O, Squadron Leader Stephenson, who I learned years later had been shot down and taken prisoner of war. We also lost Pilot Officer Watson who was seen to bale out of his aircraft over the channel but never seen again. Flying Officer Eric Ball came back slightly wounded in the arm and head but was flying again later that day. On another patrol, again on that first day, we lost another or our pilots, Sergeant Irvin, and on the same patrol Pilot Officer Lyne was shot down but made a forced landing at Deal. He was taken to hospital but didn't return to the Squadron whilst I was with it.

It was late evening when we finished work that day. After the final stand down I had to strip the guns on QV-H and give them a thorough cleaning, but no boiling, checking everything, testing the air lines and solenoids, checking the ammo boxes, testing the gun sight. This was the regular evening clean ready for the next morning's early start throughout the whole time we were at Hornchurch.

I believe every one of our aircraft that returned that day had bullet or cannon shell holes in them somewhere. I know some of them were a mass of patches by the time the riggers had finished with them! At the end of that first day we had sustained the loss of three pilots missing and two pilots wounded, and five Spitfires destroyed against the claim of 10 enemy planes destroyed. That day also saw us receive the first of a new breed of Spitfires with hydraulic operated undercarriage superseding the manual operated pump to lower and raise the undercarriage. This was on one of the replacement aircraft.

One evening after an early stand down, Stan and I were strolling around the hangars at Hornchurch when he spotted a six-inch parachute flare lying under the draped camouflage netting on the hangar. It looked abandoned so we investigated and lo and behold it still contained the cream coloured silk parachute which we quickly confiscated by cutting the shroud lines, taking care not to ignite the flare as it was live. The parachute disappeared inside Stan's tunic and within days it was at his home at Liverpool. I would like to know how many silk dresses it made for his baby daughter!

It was on May 27th, that Flight Sergeant Unwin had his first victory. That was a Hs 126, then a Me 109 on May 28th and a second 109 on June 1st, the same day that saw Sergeant Potter shot down over the Channel, although he was picked up by a fishing boat and returned to us.

Those long days, 0500 hrs until perhaps 2000 hrs, were very tiring, even if for a large part of the time we were only waiting for the Spitfires to take off or return. The weather was sunny and hot most of the time. I suppose I could say that our Squadron was lucky, as our dispersal was furthest from the main camp; just over the boundary from us was a small lake, an ideal bathing pool and 'A' Flight armourers certainly made use of it, swimming in our PT shorts. It was a way of breaking the monotony and of keeping cool.

No 222 Squadron, our old friends from Duxford, arrived on May 28th, to assist us and the other Hornchurch Squadrons and were dispersed next to us. I remember Flight Lieutenant Bader, who had by this time been promoted and posted to No 222 Squadron as a flight commander, coming across to our dispersal with Mrs Thelma Bader and Flying Officer Ball and counting the number of bullet and shell holes in Ball's Spitfire.

On June 5th we returned to Duxford having sustained no further loss of aircraft due to enemy action, but with the Squadron claiming 27 enemy aircraft destroyed and two probables. This was under the command of Flight Lieutenant Lane, who assumed temporary command after the loss of Squadron Leader Stephenson. Also that day saw us with a new C.O, Squadron Leader Pinkham, who, like Stephenson, came to us from a FTS where he had been a CFI.

Chapter Nine

DUXFORD & FOWLMERE

The Battle of Britain

On arrival back at Duxford we were all given a 48 hour pass. I was able to get away early the next morning and so didn't have that long a wait at Peterborough, got to Grimsby and was knocking on the door at Thomas Street by about 1600 hrs. What a surprise to Edna and all her family! I hadn't had time to inform them of my coming but the time soon passed and once again I was back with the Squadron.

I was informed that I was to take a trade test examination. I had heard a rumour of this before going to Grimsby. As things turned out, the exam was given by the Squadron Engineering Officer, a warrant officer, I have forgotten his name, and the entire exam was based on the Spitfire. This was a piece of cake and fortunate as I had no time to swot up on other guns or bombs or other armament. I was informed at the end of the 30 minute exam that I had passed, that was a Leading Aircraftman and could sew the propellers on my sleeves. The promotion would even be back dated to June 1st!

I am indebted to my friend and colleague, John Milne, of those far off days for the following entry. John, who was Flight Mechanic Airframe to Pilot Officer Howard Williams, recorded the following memo in his diary at the time and kindly sent me a copy.

From: Officer Commanding No 19 Squadron

To   OC A Flight
                      OC B Flight
                      OC Maintenance Flight
                      OC Squadron Armoury
                      OC Signals Section

Date 10th June 1940

Now that everyone is back and the Squadron is working on its "pre-blitz" routine, I would like to thank all personnel concerned for the work put in during the recent operations.

As the newest member of the Squadron I have heard with great interest and not a little pride of the splendid team spirit shown. Pilots and crews, maintenance personnel, and in fact the whole unit, have done extremely well and it make me confident that with this experience behind us, we will rise to even greater heights when the next show begins.

Pinkham

Squadron Leader
Commanding No 19 Squadron RAF

The Squadron, in addition to our normal patrol duties over the North Sea, now assumed a night-fighter role to combat the enemy, who was making more frequent incursions over Eastern England. This meant that all of us in turn had to do a 24 hour spell of duty. We did, of course, get our heads down in the Airmen's Rest Room in the hangar some time during the night. This duty did give us the day off the next day, not that there was much chance of rest in the Barrack Room.

The Squadron had its first night victory on the night of June 18th/19th when Flying Officer Petre engaged and shot down a Heinkel 111 at Six Mile Bottom in Cambridgeshire. Unfortunately Petre's Spitfire was hit by return fire from the Heinkel and burst into flames, badly burning the pilot. That same night Flying Officer Ball also met up with a Heinkel 111 near Margate in Kent, which he shot down, making two victories that night for the Squadron.

The following morning I was in the billiard room over at the NAAFI with Stan and a few others, having been on duty the previous night, when we saw the non-commissioned members of Petre's Heinkel being escorted back to the Guard Room after being fed in the Dining Hall. Reports filtered through to us that they were very aggressive. This was my first sight of the enemy.

On a lovely sunny morning about his time, a good friend of mine, one of the Armourers' Assistants, namely 'Ginger' Hunt, was on duty as Ground Defence Gunner in the sandbag protected Lewis gun post on the site of the old Watch Tower on the corner of the roof of what was Station Flight Hangar. In No 19 Squadron Hangar stood a fully armed Spitfire, guns all loaded and cocked, hangar doors open and by coincidence, the Spitfire's gunsight more or less aligned on the gun post. LAC Pickles, our Maintenance Flight Armourer cum 'Office Wallah' had been detailed to instruct a new member of the section, a boy entrant, Aircraftman 'Happy' Marshall, on the armament layout and the maintenance procedures on Spitfires. During his instructions to the lad, Pickles sat in the cockpit and Marshall stood on the wing root. Pickles turned the safety ring on the gun firing button.   I can imagine him with his Yorkshire accent, saying, "To fire the gun, lad, you turn this ring and press this button."   I was sitting in the Armoury chatting with some of the lads and we dropped to the floor at the noise.   The eight guns firing sounded terrific inside the hangar! We thought it was a raid! Poor Ginger Hunt, in his gun post, didn't think a lot of this. He wasn't hurt but a few of the sand bags were punctured and rumour said he had to change his trousers, but I know that not to be true!

On June 24th, 'A' and 'B' Flights were told to start packing. We were moving on 25th to Fowlmere. We were to be stationed at Manor Farm, on top of the hill overlooking the village and half a mile up the farm road from the village. This was to be a satellite station to Duxford and was code-named G1.

Flying Officer Eric Ball left us at this time, on promotion to Flight Lieutenant, to be a Flight Commander on No 242 (Hurricane) Squadron, which was now commanded by Squadron Leader Douglas Bader, our old legless pilot who had been posted from No 222 Squadron upon his own recent promotion.

When we arrived at Fowlmere the farm people were still harvesting their hay crop and some of the Squadron personnel were detailed to help to speed up the crop gathering. This was to allow the planes to land. The rest of the personnel were employed erecting bell tents, mess tents and constructing ablutions, toilets, etc also digging slit trenches, but I didn't do any digging. It was much later that each Flight had a blister hangar.

Living conditions were rough and primitive. At first our food was brought each meal time from Duxford in hay boxes to keep it hot, but later we had a mobile kitchen which was better. Fortunately, the weather at this time was kind to us, which helped. We found later that Fowlmere could be cruel on cold, wet and windy days.

The Squadron moved back to Duxford on July 3rd, being displaced at Fowlmere by No 264 Defiant Squadron, which had been reformed after their decimation at Dunkirk and now assumed a night fighter role, their Defiant aircraft being painted jet black. Little did I know then that I would be working on Defiants myself with No 151 Squadron before the year's end.

Our Squadron started receiving a new Mk1 series of Spitfires in late June. These were armed with two 20 mm Hispano cannons but no Browning guns. None of our armourers on the Squadron had any knowledge of these cannons but we had a Sergeant Thomas, a Fitter/Armourer posted to the Squadron who had been on some experimental work with cannon Spitfires elsewhere. But we saw little of this Sergeant at Fowlmere. He chose to remain at Duxford where all the talking was done, the experiments being carried out at Fowlmere.

It was on July 9th that I lost my pride and joy, Spitfire K9853 QV-H. While taxiing out for take off, Pilot Officer Howard Williams, in K9799, taxied into Flight Sergeant Unwin, in K9853, and demolished the tail and read end of the fuselage; both Spitfires were write offs. I was now to have one of the new cannon Spitfires to maintain, a new 'H for Harry'. Not having any knowledge of the Hispano cannon or its working, and with no printed information to guide us, didn't make maintenance any too easy and, being of an experimental installation, the cannon weren't working properly in the Spitfires; the pilots were having a lot of stoppages during air firing practice at the Sutton Bridge air firing range.

Myself from 'A' Flight and a LAC from 'B' Flight (I can't remember who) were sent on July 15th to No 1 AAS at RAF Manby on a one-week 20 mm cannon course. Unfortunately, other than being given names to all the parts of the cannon, we knew more about the gun than the instructors did! This short interlude at Manby, so near Grimsby, gave me a chance to see Edna. There was no school on the Saturday of my week in Lincolnshire, so I was off to Grimsby. We spent the day together at Cleethorpes and I recall now that we couldn't walk on the beach. It was barbed wire fenced off with mine warnings and we were restricted to the promenade. I did tell her that I could possibly be having seven days leave in the near future and we agreed to make plans for her to visit my home in Wales and meet my parents with me.

There had been no further success in reducing the stoppages on the cannons by our fellow armourers by the time we returned from Manby, despite the many experiments carried out. 'A' and 'B' Flights moved back to Fowlmere on July 25th, and from there flew daily to Coltishall from where they flew convoy patrols. No 264 Squadron had left Fowlmere and transferred their base to RAF Kirton-in-Lindsey.

We still had some eight-gun Spitfires on the Squadron strength which was fortunate because the cannon stoppages seemed to be unsolvable. Most of the trouble stemmed from the cannons being mounted on their sides, therefore the empty shell cases were being ejected sideways from the breech and deflected back into the breech. Also the shells were not always entering the breech. The nose of the shell dropping slightly and striking the breech end of the barrel and causing the shell case to buckle at the neck and this causing another kind of stoppage. We fitted various types of deflector plates. We altered the angle of the plates, we fitted rubber pads to dampen the force of the spent shell case, but none of these experiments worked. We also have magazine feed trouble. This was caused by the magazine lying on its side while mounted on the cannon. To counter this one, we tried varying the tension we applied to the magazine spring but this wasn't successful.

We took a lot of stick from the pilots over these stoppages. For a while they wanted to blame the armourers for the trouble and then, when a full magazine of 20 mm ammunition was expended, the pilots complained that they only had six seconds of firing time against the 18 seconds with the Browning guns. We had little help and no encouragement from our armament staff at Duxford. In fact, Sergeant Thomas, who was supposed to guide us, we saw very little of. Even the experts who came from RAF Northolt to help us could only listen and learn from. We were taken by lorry to Duxford two or perhaps three times a week to bathe and visit the NAAFI to get any supplies we needed such as toothpaste, soap, etc, there being no canteen at Fowlmere, and I can't remember there being a shop in the village. We were leg-pulled by our maintenance armourers left at Duxford about our spartan existence but I think they were envious of us. We had none of the barrack room bull and we were where all the action was taking place.

It was difficult finding our way round in the dark at night as there was no illumination of any kind. I did have an old torch in my possession but no batteries. These couldn't be purchased anywhere. I solved the problem by begging a 120 volt high tension dry battery from the Signal Section; then, breaking the battery down into separate cells, I wound newspaper around each of two cells to make them fit the torch, a 2.5 volt bulb and 'hey presto' it worked! The 80 cells in that battery lasted me all the following winter. These 120 volt batteries were used in the aircraft radio but were changed, and the used battery returned to stores when the voltage dropped to 110 volts. I think the battery I acquired must have been written off as 'lost in transit'.

Towards the end of July we had a few days of terrible weather, the rain and the winds were horrendous, our tents were flooded until we dug drainage trenches around them. Our clothes were damp and we couldn't dry them. We were glad to see the sunshine again! While it was so windy we had to run out to the centre of the airfield to meet the aircraft as they landed and sit on the tail unit while the plane was taxied to the dispersal area. Then we had to rope them down to screw pickets by both wings and tail. I think we had two aircraft blown onto their noses before we could get to them in one particular gale; there was definitely one with Sergeant Jack Potter in the cockpit.

We first became operational with the cannon Spitfires on July 22nd, this despite the recurring stoppages and carried on with the convoy patrols although a massive fight was raging further south between Nos 11 and 10 Group Squadrons and the *Luftwaffe* No 11 Group's airfields in particular were taking a pounding from the German Bombers.

I was granted leave from after duty on Friday, August 9th to 2359 hrs on August 17th. I travelled to London, leaving Whittlesford about midnight, and with other servicemen was allowed to stay on the train at Liverpool Street Station until about 0630 hrs when the empty coaches were moved, so I had a few hours sleep. I met Edna at Kings Cross station about 1100 hrs and we travelled to South Wales from Paddington. I think we arrived at my home in Neath about 1900 hrs. Of course the first hour or so was all introductions, aunts, uncles, cousins, all those living near had to call. There is none so nosy as the Welsh; my mother must have spent all the previous day telling of our impending visit. It was embarrassing to both of us but that is the Welsh way, we are a nosy nation!

We had a glorious week. I remember the weather was hot and sunny every day. We visited the Gower beaches. We walked the hills and mountains, we were never idle. It was Edna's first holiday anywhere outside of Lincolnshire. The highlight of the holiday to me was presenting Edna to my Grandmother Parkin; to know her approval was given, nothing else mattered. The week soon passed and we were on the train, on our way back again. I put Edna on the Grimsby train at Kings Cross and got back to Duxford late evening. I managed to beg a lift to Fowlmere, arriving there before dark to find things much as I had left it.

I was told that while I had been away 'B' Flight, led by our the Squadron C.O, Squadron Leader Pinkham, had been detached to RAF Eastchurch on August 12th, the groundstaff flying there in a Bristol Bombay transport aircraft. Eastchurch airfield was bombed at about 0730 hrs on August 13th by a Do 17, which dropped about 200 bombs. There were a large number of RAF ground staff killed and wounded during the attack, but fortunately none were 19 Squadron personnel. On their return to Fowlmere on August 14th, Eastchurch being temprarily unusable, our 'B' Flight colleagues told the rest of the Squadron of the dead and wounded and of the shambles they had left behind them at Eastchurch.

The cannon shells we used in our Hispano cannons were of two types, ball and high explosive (H.E). The H.E shell was highly decorated, being enamelled in rings of about four different colours. This looked pretty and I suppose would have made a good ornament. That is what paddy O'Brennan thought. He was trying to de-fuse an H.E shell one day in August by holding the shell in a bucket water and filing off the nose-cap, so that he could take out the fulminate of mercury explosive pellet. Several of us warned him and criticised him. This shouldn't have been necessary, as Paddy was one of our pre-war armourers, but the inevitable happened. The shell exploded and blew off half his hand.

On returning from that leave I was also pleased to learn that my pilot, Flight Sergeant Unwin, had been in action with my new Mk1B Spitfire with two cannons and four browning guns.

I spent a lot of time sunbathing once the aircraft had taken off for Coltishall or further test firing of the cannons at Sutton Bridge. There was little to do. There was the occasional scramble for whichever flight was left at Fowlmere, but no action, not until August 24th when the Squadron took off in the afternoon and were vectored onto a large formation of Me 109s and Me 110s. In the ensuing scrap, Flight Lieutenant Lane shot down an Me 110 and Sergeant Jennings shot down two. On the same day, we received our first Czech pilots. These turned out to be exceptional pilots but they were impatient. There again, they had reason to want to get at the Germans. They had lost families, homes and country.

August 31st dawned bright and clear. It was a beautiful sunny morning and at about 0800 hrs our Squadron was scrambled to cover RAF Debden, where they met a force of *Luftwaffe* fighters and bombers. In the ensuing action, due to more cannon stoppages, we lost three Spitfires, Flying Officer Coward being severely wounded and baling out, Flying Officer Brinsden taking to his parachute but landing unhurt, and Pilot Officer Aerberhardt, whilst attempting to land at Fowlmere without flaps, crashed and was burned to death. This we all witnessed but could do nothing to help.

At about 0830 hrs, while the Squadron was away, I was in the breakfast queue at Fowlmere, knife, fork, spoon and enamel plate in hand. The village air raid siren had sounded an imminent air raid warning when someone shouted. "They're nearly overhead!" Looking up I could see these planes which I learned later were Dornier 17s. There were about 30 of them. I could see them shining in the sun. I could also see the bombs dropping! A quick dive into the nearby slit trench along with the others and I remember sitting there holding my enamel plate over my head. I don't know what protection it would have given. Fortunately for us the bombs had been released late, only one bomb landing on the airfield and this among our bell tents. It exploded, making a crater four feet deep and five feet across. A second bomb exploded just beyond the boundary fence, and a few more in the nearby orchards and watercress beds. We had no casualties but John and Jimmy Belton were still in bed and had the tent they were in blown on top of them; they were half buried with earth from the bomb crater!

One piece of good fortune came to us as the result of the Luftwaffe visit. The local landowner and farmer came up to the boundary fence soon after the raid and presented the boys with a large sack of eating applies. These had been blown off the trees in his orchards by the exploding bombs and he told us to help ourselves to any more that were on the ground, but to please leave the few that were remaining on the trees. Most of the bombs that were dropped in the raid fell in the vicinity of Shepreth and Meldreth villages.

Flight Sergeant Unwin wasn't flying that morning, Spitfire R6776 being grounded for routine maintenance. I remember just after the raid Sergeant Jennings returning in a hurry as he couldn't get any oxygen: his Flight Rigger had failed to turn on the oxygen supply in the fuselage. This was quickly rectified and he was off again to look for the Squadron. The Dorniers that raided Fowlmere were later found and attacked by No 111 (Hurricane) Squadron as they headed for the coast.

Everyone on our Squadron felt sure that had we eight-gun Spitfires our pilots could have achieved much more than the two Me 110s they shot down that morning, and probably not have lost the three aircraft and two pilots.

The Squadron was now being called on much more often as the raids were on London and the south-east towns, instead of airfields, and were becoming more frequent and heavy. We ground staff regularly gatherered around any spare aircraft after our planes had taken off and listened to the dialogue between pilots and pilots, pilots and control while our aircraft were engaged with the enemy. This dialogue was conveyed to us by one of the Wireless Operators from the Signal Section who was listening on the spare aircraft radio. This also gave us an indication of the time of return of the aircraft and, in some cases, the state of the aircraft and pilot.

More action on September 3rd and 5th, but sadly on 5th we lost our C.O, Squadron leader Pinkham, who was shot down over Kent. He baled out severely wounded but was too low for his parachute to open properly and he was later found dead. Flight Lieutenant Lane was promoted that same day to the rank of Squadron Leader and assumed command of the Squadron. All our Mk1B cannon-armed Spitfires were withdrawn on September 6th. It was ironic that this should happen just one day after Squadron Leader Pinkham was killed when, for so long he had pleaded for the withdrawal of the MK1B Spitfires because of their unreliable armament We had these Mk1B aircraft replaced by a lot of old Mk1A Spitfires that were flown from an OTU at RAF Hawarden by pilots of the Air Transport Auxiliary, some of them lady pilots.

The OTU personnel must have selected their worse aircraft to send to us. I know the aircraft flew but only just, and the armament was in a terrible state. It was a good thing No 611 Squadron had been flown to Fowlmere that day to provide cover whilst we made the exchange because the armament in these replacement aircraft had been badly maintained. They had rusty gun barrels, fouled up muzzle chokes, lack of oiling, we even found ammunition tanks so badly buckled that the ammunition belts wouldn't have run smoothly and would have caused stoppages. I could carry on listing the faults we found, and the other trades found faults equally as glaring. The planes certainly had not had the high standard of maintenance that everyone gave on No 19 Squadron.

I consider myself to have been very fortunate as my cannon Spitfire, R6776, was flown to Hendon by Flight Sergeant Unwin who returned with a brand new Mk1A eight-gun Spitfire, P9546, and this became our new QV-H. The next day, September 7th, saw us become part of the Duxford Wing. This consisted of No 19 (Spitfire) Squadron, No 310 Czech (Hurricane) Squadron and No 242 (Hurricane) Squadron, the Wing being led by Squadron Leader Douglas Bader of 242. On this day I remember that the Wing was in action three times and accounted for a number of enemy planes without loss.

That same week also saw us lose one of our long serving pilots. Sergeant Jack Potter was shot down near the French coast on September 11th, and I read 50 years later that he was taken prisoner of war. September 11th also saw Flight Sergeant Unwin attack a Dornier over London in P9546, but he was shot down himself and made a wheels-down forced landing near Brentwood in Essex. The plane was repaired and George flew it back to Duxford two days later, but the windscreen, which had been penetrated, couldn't be repaired there and so the Spitfire was flown away. Another QV-H gone and after only nine days! This aircraft was replaced by another brand new Mk1A, Spitfire X4179, another QV-H.

One afternoon, whilst I still maintained P9546, the aircraft was up on trestles in the 'A' Flight blister hangar when a scramble took place. The engine cowlings were off, the gun fairings were off, the guns were unloaded and the ammo tanks removed. The Flight Mech's Engine and Airframe and myself were all at work when Flight Sergeant Unwin came running and yelling for his plane. I'm sure we must have broken a record for bringing a Spit to serviceability after that first shout from him! George was airborne in less than 10 minutes and after the rest of the Squadron with a straight take-off across the wind and no engine warm-up. I don't know if he caught up with them or took the *Luftwaffe* on his own, but it showed the courage of the man and the confidence he placed in us, his ground crew.

There was jubilation in 'A' Flight on September 17th when we heard that Flight Sergeant Unwin had been awarded the Distinguished Flying Medal. We, his ground crew, were really proud. He had earned it for us. Up to date George had shot down 12 enemy aircraft.

The following day No 616 Squadron came to Fowlmere from Kirton-in-Lindsey to take part in the Duxford Wing, which would then consist of five Squadrons. I remember them returning to us at Fowlmere for re-fuelling and re-arming after seeing action and one of their young pilots reviling the No 616 armourers, who were of course at Lindsey, and threatening all sorts of dire consequences on his return there because his eight guns had stopped firing almost immediately he pressed the firing button. On examination we found the fault and, on questioning the officer, he admitted he was flying upside down when he fired and hadn't thought, in the heat of the moment, that the spent cartridge cases wouldn't be properly ejected when the guns were upside down and would fall back between the breechblock and the barrel, jamming the guns. There was a very red faced officer and a lot of leg pulling by his fellow pilots of No 616 Squadron. I think he did admit to lack of experience and I did wonder if the armourers at Kirton-in-Lindsey ever heard of his outburst.

Throughout this period at Fowlmere we weren't altogether without relaxation. After duty on several evening a weeks we would make our way to the village where we were always made welcome by mine host and the village people at the 'Black Horse'. We were not so welcome at the 'Chequers', the opposite side of the village street; the landlord there had a social chip on his shoulder because our pilots frequented his pub. Of course beer was in short supply at this time so there were occasions when we would arrived to find a 'no beer' sign on the door. We also found a great welcome in the little canteen in the village, run by those wonderful ladies of the local Women's Voluntary Service who sold home-made cakes and scones, sausage rolls and pasties. Goodness knows where they obtained the ingredients, remember everything was rationed in those days, but all this we appreciated, bearing in mind we had no NAAFI at Fowlmere, other than the mobile canteen that came from Duxford every mid morning with tea, cakes and cigarettes.

We had photographers descend on us at Fowlmere on September 21st. I believe they came from the Ministry of Information or Defence. We ground staff had to pose for them, carrying out different duties. Spitfire X4474 QV-I was chosen for this purpose with Sergeant Jennings in the cockpit. He was the regular pilot of this aircraft though there were some photographs taken of other aircraft, including one of QV-K, the C.O's Spitfire, with Charlie Stanley and myself working on the wing.

I'm given to understand that the photograph taken of me re-arming X4474 QV-I was to become rather famous, but I must emphasise that re-arming Spitfires was a team job and not a solo effort. In any case although I was supposed to be re-arming QV-I, it was not my aircraft. I was Flight Sergeant Unwins' Armourer and my aircraft was QV-H.

Just after this Charlie Stanley was promoted to Corporal and posted to Bomber Command. I did miss him. We had been mates from our first introduction in July 1939, and had worked so much together as a team. Out of the original eight pre-war armourers on the Squadron only Jimmy Belton, Clappy Clayton and I were left at Fowlmere.

Sunday, September 22nd and it was early afternoon, the local siren had sound an air raid warning. 'Red Roofs' Section had taken off and I think all of us were in the slit trenches then a Do 17 shot out of the low clouds from the direction of Great Chishill and flew directly over 'B' Flight dispersal. He dropped 10 bombs and destroyed a Spitfire, X4351. I can't remember how I came to have a rifle in my hands on this occasion but remember I just had time to fire one round at the Dornier and that was tracer, the only .303 round I had in my pocket at the time. Several of the other lads who had rifles handy also took pot shots, but I don't think we did any damage.

The *Dornier* was directly over 'B' Flight dispersal when 'Red Roofs' Section came out of the clouds behind him in line astern. 'Red Roofs' Leader opened fire but with no result as the *Dornier* escaped. One incident I remember seeing during the raid was the RAF ground gunner, with a Lewis gun on top of the pill box at 'A' Flight Dispersal opening fire, and keeping on firing at the *Dornier*, whilst his counterpart at 'B' Flight, on seeing the *Dornier*, jumped down and fled inside the pill box!

We started having our Mk I Spitfires replaced towards the end of September with the new Mk II aircraft. These were fitted with a more powerful Rolls Royce Merlin engine and Koffman Cartridge Starters, no more lugging around those heavy accumulator trolleys from aircraft to aircraft at scrambles. Then in early October, a Spitfire armed with two cannons and four Browning guns, and a new belt feed mechanism, was delivered to Duxford.

One very windy night in October, after blackout, I was in the 'Black Horse', which was fairly full. I knew there were some

German bombers about because the air raid sirens had sounded and I had heard their engines. Someone rushed into the bar and shouted, "There is a parachute mine hanging in the tree at the back of the pub!" The pub was empty in about 10 seconds flat! We never even bothered to find out if it was true! We were out of the village in double quick time and back to camp. Next day we were told that it was a bed sheet from someone's washing line in the village that had been blown into the tree by the near gale force wind!

During our long stay at Fowlmere, guard duties on the airfield were carried out by the army and at that time, I believe, by the Cameron Highlanders. One night in October, at about 2300 hrs, the whole of the Squadron's ground staff were roused from our tents by the Squadron Duty Officer and lined up for an identity parade. Some irregularity had occurred between an airman returning to camp and the Sentry of the approach road from the village, and then the Airman had run off. This had been reported to the Guard Commander by the Sentry and so the resulting identity parade. Unfortunately Jim Belton was picked out by the Sentry as the culprit and, despite his protestations, was placed under open arrest by our Duty Officer. We armourers knew this not to be true and that it was a case of mistaken identity because Jim hadn't been out of camp all evening, and had actually been in his bed at least since 2130 hrs. In fact none of the armourers had been out that evening. I don't know what happened to Jim or what resulted from the incident. Jim had plenty of witnesses to his whereabouts that evening, but I left the Squadron soon after and never heard what happened.

On October 20th, I was told to report to the Squadron Armoury at Duxford, and was there informed that I would be leaving on the following day on a short detachment to No 151 (Hurricane) Squadron at RAF North Weald. They had an experimental Hurricane armed with two Hispano cannons on their strength and need assistance with the maintenance.

Chapter Ten

DIGBY, BRAMCOTE & WITTERING

The Blitz

Many an evening after dark in late September and October 1940, I stood on our hill top airfield at Fowlmere and looked south-east, to London 40 miles away. I tried to form a mind's eye view of the intense bombing that the Londoners were enduring. I could see from our elevated position the search-lights probing the sky around the city, searching for the *Luftwaffe*, the hundreds of flashes of AA shells exploding, the larger flashes of the bombs exploding on the ground and the false sunset made by the fires that lasted the entire nights and lit up the whole southern sky.

It was on my train journey to Liverpool Street Station that the extent of the damage that was being done by the bombing that I had seen from a distance was brought home to me.

During my journey through the capital in August, there had been no damage to see. Then, the *Luftwaffe* was concentrating attacks on airfields by daylight. Now it was night and indiscriminate bombing. I was horrified to see such destruction all the way from the northern outskirts into the city and out again on the train to North Weald.

I presented my movement documents at the Guard Room at RAF North Weald, from where I was conducted to the Station Headquarters. There I was immediately informed that No 151 Squadron was no longer there. They had left North Weald on September 1st and enquiries would be made to ascertain their whereabouts at this time.

I was at North Weald about two hours, which was enough time to have a meal and see the damage that had been inflicted by a recent bombing raid on the camp. The camp was virtually wiped out. I wasn't given time to see everything before I was told that No 151 Squadron was then based at RAF Digby, in Lincolnshire, andgiven a Railway Station Warrant and Travel Instructions to proceed there, plus the usual cheese sandwiches and an apple.

It was after dark when I arrived at Lincoln Railway Station and reported to the Railway Transport Office (RTO) on the railway station. After a wait I was given transport along with several other airmen to Digby. There I was given a meal and then conducted to a barrack block where I was given a bed for the night and instructed to report to the Squadron Headquarters, which had been pointed out to me, on the following morning.

I was given accommodation the next morning with No 151 Squadron Maintenance Flight Armourer. 'A' and 'B' Flight personnel were accommodated in huts at their respective dispersal areas. I was then taken to the Squadron Armoury and introduced to everyone. I was told that the cannon armed Hurricane I was to service had been flown to Digby on October 10th by Flight Lieutenant Smith, from RAF Martlesham Heath, where it had been stored in a hangar after some experimental work. This same Hurricane, L1750, had been with the Squadron earlier in the year. I was also told that the Squadron had a four-cannon Hurricane on its strength earlier in 1940; this aircraft had also been flown by Flight Lieutenant Smith, with some little success against the *Luftwaffe*, before being flown away for further experiments.

I found that Hurricane L1750 had its cannons, one each side, suspended below the main planes, where the eight Browning guns were normally fitted, and covered with fairings for a pod. Access to the breech of the cannons, to carry out maintenance and to fit the two 60-round magazines was through the top of the main planes. The two cannons on L1750 had been fired but not been properly cleaned afterwards, although were not in a particularly bad state of maintenance. I was given the assistance of another armourer and I believe we spent four or perhaps five days removing and stripping down the cannons. We gave them a thorough cleaning, removing the list rust we found, gauging and testing everything, then re-assembling the cannons. We re-fitted the cannons to the aircraft but before they were harmonised with the gun sight or butt-fired we were told to lock-nut and wire everything up. A few days later L1750 was flown away, but I have no recollection of where it went.

It seemed my little expertise was no longer needed at No 151 Squadron and with my task completed I immediately asked that I be allowed to return to No 19 Squadron. A day later I was informed that my detachment had been made a permanent posting and I was then on No 151 strength.

50 years later, on receipt of my Service Records, which I had requested from the Royal Air Force Records Office, I found that I had indeed been posted back to No 19 Squadron on December 9th, 1940, and the records even show my arrival back on the Squadron! Why I was never told of this at the time, or allowed to go, I will never know, or how they could record my arrival back on No 19 Squadron, when I never returned there.

I explained to the Orderly Room Sergeant, however, that nearly half of my kit was still at Fowlmere and after a mild rebuke was given a day off to travel to Fowlmere and collect it at my own expense. This I did by hitch hiking to Fowlmere.

On my arrival I found that in my absence the ground staff had been moved from the tents and were now accommodated in huts. The armourers, I found, had made their home in the Manor Farm barn, and John had been kind enough to take care of my kit during the move and for the whole of my absence from No 19 Squadron. It was all as I had left it in my kitbag. An hour or so of reminiscence with my old colleagues and I was on my way back to Digby, taking advantage of an RAF lorry going my way which put me on the A1 road going to North Weald.

I remember sitting by the tailboard of that lorry as we drove away from Fowlmere and thinking of how I was going to miss all those fine people I had lived with and worked with the last 16 months, all the riggers and mechanics, the signal and instrument personnel and most of all, the armourers, especially Charlie Stanley and Happy Marshall. I knew I was going to miss the Spitfires and the No 19 Squadron pilots, Flight Sergeant Unwin and his dog 'Flash', and Sergeant Jennings with whom I had shared the photograph. Then there was Flight Sergeant Steer and Sergeant Cox, Flying Officer Brinsden, Sub-Lieutenant Blake ('The Admiral') of the Fleet, Air Arm and, of course, Squadron Leader Lane, on whose aircraft I had so often worked with Charlie Stanley, and all the other members of 'A' and 'B' Flights.

I mention the N.C.O pilots with emphasis because they were much closer to us, having been through the ranks themselves. They were all excellent people to work with. I know all the pilots of No 19 Squadron, commissioned and non-commissioned, fully appreciated the efforts of the ground crews, at all times, to keep the Squadron at as high a pitch of efficiency as possible, often under difficult circumstances. I would like to say that the young commissioned pilots that came to the Squadron later in 1940 hadn't the same character as the older officers and appeared to be stand-offish, but reflecting this in my old age, I think they might have been shy or frightened of us, we were, after all, the old hands.

I made my way back to Digby via Huntingdon, Stamford and Sleaford, being very fortunate with lifts, even sharing one lorry driver's sandwiches!

I should state that No 151 Squadron had assumed the role of night fighters on their moving to Digby, a role I believe they held in the 1914 - 1918 war. The Squadron was known as the 'Owl Squadron', because the Squadron crest depicted an owl. The Squadron's Commanding Officer at this time was Squadron Leader West.

The next day I was allocated to 'A' Flight of No 151 Squadron and had to leave the barrack block and move across the airfield to the Dispersal. 'A' Flight hut was as far from the main camp as was possible within the perimeter of the airfield. I think there were about 30 of us in that hut. I remember it was crowded. The lads consisted of mechanics, riggers and armourers. We were transported three times a day to and from the Dining Hall for meals and there was frequent transport circling the perimeter to take personnel to the main camp, for the NAAFI or stores or to take a bath etc.

The first thing I noticed on entering 'A' Flight's hut was the huge pot simmering on the coke burning stove that heated the hut. It could easily have held five gallons of liquid, in this case chicken and mushroom soup. I was offered a mug of this soup which I gratefully accepted. I was told that the chicken was reared locally and freshly killed the previous day and the mushrooms were picked that morning on the airfield. There was a poultry farm adjacent to Digby's satellite airfield, code name L1, from where the Squadron operated at night. And this farm contained several thousand of what we call today, free range poultry. Part of 'A' Flight's night duty crew's unofficial duties while at L1 was to ensure that some of the birds didn't range so far in the night. There were foxes about of course, most nights while we were there, and, as nature decreed, one or two birds would be carried away (to Digby). We never heard of any birds being missed. That chicken farm also ensured that any of 'A' Flight airmen going on leave or pass was able to take a few fresh eggs home. I can only remember spending two nights at L1 myself. One of those nights it poured with rain, so the two Hurricanes we had there were bogged down and couldn't even taxi, so there was no possibility of taking off. It was a horrible place to be on a winter's night.

Our Hurricanes were parked close to the Dispersal at Digby, so there was very little walking to work and being so far from the hangars we had no "Bull", but we had to don ties to attend meals or the NAAFI or headquarters, no roll-neck jerseys there!

I found I was the only pre-war armourer on the Flight, the others were either VR or conscripted servicemen. I was to find the conscripts at the time didn't have the same dedication as the others. It was always, "Let the others do it," attitude with them, which made for unpleasantness, something I had never encountered before. We didn't have any conscripted men on No 19 Squadron armament staff and No 151 didn't have the No 19 Squadron system where we each had our own aircraft and or own guns to maintain and take pride in.

I found the Mk I and Mk IIA Hurricanes easy aircraft to maintain as regards armament, everything being accessible from the top of the wing with plenty of room to work. But despite four top panels, four bottom panels and two ammunition recess panels in each wing, plus limited access giving to cut fingers, numerous sore heads through bumping, wet trousers through kneeling in wet grass, leading to rheumatism in the knees (with which I still suffer today), I still think of the Spitfire with a lot of love and will always say it was the greatest aircraft of its time. The Hurricane was a good aircraft, however, and highly praised by those that flew in it. It was a wonderfully manoeuvrable aircraft and a great gun platform with its close concentration of four guns each side, which was better than the Spitfire's spread of fire.

On night at Digby, we were woken after midnight by a burst of machine-gun fire close at hand. This was the time when there were frequent invasion alerts in England. On rushing out to seek the cause of the gunfire we found that some nervous and trigger-happy soldiers of the Airfield Defence Unit, in a nearby gun pit, had been alarmed by rustling and movement in a hedgerow; not receiving a reply to their challenge they opened fire. The poor sheep that had wandered out of their field didn't stand a chance against the heavily armed soldiers! I don't know how many sheep were killed or had to be destroyed, but it was said there was a lot of mutton eaten in the army camp and the three Digby messes afterwards.

I can't recall the Squadron having any action during my time with it at Digby, but we did lose several Hurricanes on training flights. A particularly bad incident occurred on October 26th, when two pilots collided after take off, one being killed instantly, the other dying the next day.

It was early November that I managed a 72-hour pass and made a beeline for Grimsby. Being so near to Digby, I managed to hitch hike both ways easily. It was good to see Edna again. This was the first time since I had seen her onto the train at Kings Cross in August, but I considered I was more fortunate than a good many airmen who were being posted abroad.

Grimsby was changing every time I visited. It seemed less full of civilians and fuller of naval personnel and airmen. Of course it was an important North Sea Naval base and there were numerous RAF airfield and bombing ranges in the area. Like all good things, the 72 hours soon passed and I was back on the Squadron, back in the dispersal hut, back to the usual night standbys and day time training and patrols.

I left Digby, along with the rest of No 151 Squadron ground staff, on November 28th, for RAF Bramcote in Warwickshire. This airfield was quite new and was about three miles from Nuneaton. We travelled by motor coach and I well remember arriving there. All the ground staff was allocated a barrack block that had been vacated by the personnel of No 18 (Polish) OTU, which flew Wellington bombers. In entering the rooms it was like entering a present day Boots perfumery department; I know the Polish airmen had a reputation for bravery, but we wondered if this lot were a load of poofter heroes or whether they shared the rooms with a detachment of WAAFs!

Coventry had suffered its big *Blitz* on November 15th, and now Birmingham and other Midland towns were being raided nightly. We were told our move to Bramcote as a night-fighter unit was to situate us nearer the raiders' flight path.

It was during our stay at Bramcote that we started to change our Hurricanes for Boulton and Paul Defiant two-seater fighters, which had a four-gun power-operated turret in the rear, but no forward-firing armament. This also meant that we now had air gunners on the strength of the Squadron.

Our stay at Bramcote was of short duration. Whilst there we did have difficulty night flying because of our close proximity to Coventry; considering the heavy bombing the people had suffered, the local population were frightened and didn't want anything to lead the raiders to them again, so every time our ground staff lit the goose-necked flares and switched on the Chance-light to allow our Hurricane or Defiants to take off or land, the local Home Guard took pot shots at the flares with their rifles. This made the Flare Path Party's job rather hazardous. This might have been the reason why our stay there was ended so quickly, but we left, again by coach, on December 22nd, 1940. This time we were to be located at RAF Wittering. This airfield was situated about three miles south of Stamford in Lincolnshire and on the Lincolnshire/ Cambridgeshire border.

Before I leave Bramcote I must mention that we found the residents of Nuneaton very hospitable. We were invited into their homes and accepted into their families on every possible opportunity. I attended dances at the Cooperative Hall in Nuneaton on two occasions. I still couldn't dance, but the beer, Flowers Ale, was good and because we were a fighter squadron and based locally the beer was mostly free!

Wittering was a very old and established airfield so we were billeted in barrack blocks. I wouldn't have liked to have been in wooden huts for the following months as it was to be a hard winter. The Station C.O was Group Captain Harry Broadhurst, and we shared the station with No 25 Squadron, which flew Blenheims and Beaufighters and, like No 151 Squadron, were night-fighters, and No 266 Squadron which flew Spitfires and were a day fighter Squadron.

It was around this time that we were to have a new Squadron C.O, Squadron Leader West was to leave us and our new C.O was Squadron Leader Adams. Also, Group Captain Broadhurst was to relinquish command of the Station about this time and hand over command to Group Captain Basil Embry.

We continued to convert to a Defiant Squadron but retained some Hurricanes, one to be flown by the C.O, Squadron Leader Adams, and one to be flown by Pilot Officer Stevens. This pilot wouldn't fly Defiants. He was an ex-civilian pilot and flew night mail around Europe pre-war. He had lost his wife and children in the blitz and held a personal vendetta with the *Luftwaffe*.

Christmas 1940 was with us and despite shortages of food elsewhere we did rather well at Wittering. We had the traditional turkey and roast served by the officers and senior N.C.Os of the station, with a pre-meal speech by the Station Commander, and had a quiet night, the Germans leaving us in peace.

The evening of January 1st, saw Jerry visit us, however. A single aircraft came across our flare-path and dropped four 50 kg bombs. These exploded at the rear of No 25 Squadron Hangar but only damaged the boiler house and coal compound. We were very fortunate, perhaps he didn't have any more bombs to drop. It found work for the 'Janker Wallahs', shovelling up coal and cleaning up the mess that had been created!

With the start of the New Year, the Station Commander, Group Captain, Captain Embry, thought that the whole of the station personnel were in a sorry state of physical fitness and decreed that everyone not on essential duties at 0630 hrs was to attend 30 minutes of physical training on the square every morning, officers and N.C.Os included. This didn't go down well with the other ranks and I believe caused some mutinous thoughts in the Officers' and Sergeants' Messes, but physical training we did in the worse of the weather. To me, these exercises came hard. I hadn't participated in any physical training since leave Uxbridge 18 months earlier. I, like a lot of my colleagues had gone soft. I can't remember which but this PT business faded out after a couple of weeks, perhaps it was causing discontent among the hierarchy.

It was on the night of January 15th/16th that Pilot Officer Stevens had a double success in his Hurricane, shooting down a Do 17 and a He 111. This was the first occasion that a fighter pilot had accounted for two of the *Luftwaffe* in one night. Of course the Squadron and Station were jubilant at this result.

I had been on duty three nights running one period in January, and on the fourth evening, being off duty, I made a visit to a cinema in Peterborough. I can't recall the film but it starred Errol Flynn. Anyway, tired as I was, I fell asleep in the cinema and was woken by the attendant after the audience had all left and found that I had missed the last bus to Wittering. I had to walk some miles before I managed to get a lift. I was some hours adrift when I arrived back at camp and was charged as such by the RAF Police. My explanation to the Squadron C.O, Squadron Leaders Adams, wasn't believed. He insisted

I had been somewhere with a woman. I was punished with three days CB (Confined to Barracks), not, he said, for being adrift but for telling lies.

CB consisted of reporting to the Guard Room each day at 1800 hrs in best blue uniform and full pack. After inspection by the Orderly Officer, changing into work dress and carrying out duties as allocated by the Officer, i.e. cook house fatigues, then reporting again to the guard room at 2200 hrs, again in best blue uniform and full pack, and again the same the following morning at 0600 hrs for each of day of punishment.

With the aid of the Senior Armament N.C.O on the Squadron I side tracked most of this punishment by volunteering three extra night duties on the dispersal, concurrently with the CB, so I only had to report to the guard room at 1800 hrs. I was on Squadron Duties at the dispersal the remainder of each of the three nights.

The winter of 1941 was to be terrible. I am sure it was colder than 1940. I know there was six inches or more on snow on Wittering airfield on my 21st birthday on February 17th, and we spent most of the day clearing the snow off the field to allow the planes to take off and land. I remember being at dispersal when the mail arrived. This included a fruit cake made by my mother, goodness knows where she obtained the ingredients, but shared among my greed fellow armourers it lasted about 10 minutes and was washed down with NAAFI tea when the van visited us. I also had a birthday card from Edna with birthday wishes but to my surprise nothing else. I can't recall all my exact thoughts at this, but do recall feeling rather sad.

Several other armourers and I from 151 Squadron were sent to the Boulton and Paul Aircraft Factory at Wolverhampton late in February, on a Boulton and Paul gun turret course. These were the gun turrets fitted in the Defiant aircraft. We were to stay at a boarding house near to the Wolverhampton Football Ground and we travelled to and from the factory each day by public transport from Queens Square in Wolverhampton. The course was interesting and was conducted by a flying officer of ground staff who was based at the factory. There was no examination at the end of the course, but I believe there was an assessment by the tutor.

I had written to Edna telling her of my temporary move to Wolverhampton, but on my return to Wittering a letter awaited me from her accusing me of preferring to go to Wolverhampton rather than Grimsby and saying it would be better that we terminated our friendship. I believe this decision had been in her mind on my last visit to Grimsby, but an excuse hadn't occurred then or she couldn't face me and tell me. I don't know if there was someone else and despite writing several letters I never heard from Edna again

Edna's stepsister communicated with my mother until my mother died in the 1950s. By this means I learned that Edna was eventually directed to war work at the Rolls Royce factory at Derby, married someone there and they emigrated to South Africa after the war finished. But I never did learn the true reason for finishing our friendship.

On the night of February 4th/5th, the Squadron celebrated our first victory with a Defiant, Sergeant Bodien, the pilot and

Sergeant Jones, the gunner shooting down a Do 17, but we lost a Defiant on the night of February 23rd/24th. This plane was abandoned running short of fuel, and one of the crew was killed.

Early March I had a long weekend leave and, no longer having to go to Grimsby, I hitchhiked to Norwich. I stayed at a boarding house in the city centre. While I was there I saw an Austin Seven 1931 car advertised for sale at the ridiculously low price of £15, with petrol coupons. I bought the car, got myself a driving licence (no tests during the war) and insurance and drove myself back to Wittering. I don't know how I did it, I had never driven a car before. My little driving experience had been on tractors on the airfields.

We had many a happy hour with that car on the Squadron. I had the brake cables renewed with Hurricane control cables and it ran wonderfully well on Chore Horse petrol, and at a squeeze it could carry five of us to and from Peterborough or Stamford. The Chore Horse was a little petrol engine fitted on top of the aircraft started accumulator trolley and drove the generator that charged the accumulators.

We were bombed again on the night of March 14th/15th, six 250kg high explosive bombs and approximately 100 incendiary bombs being dropped this time. One bomb dropped through the roof of No 25 Squadron hangar, and through a Beaufighter, a second bomb exploded in the roof of the hangar causing widespread damage. The other high explosive bombs exploding on in the Airmen's Dining Hall and the Officers' Mess causing tremendous damage. The incendiaries set fire

to a hangar and the Station Cinema and two barrack blocks.
There were three men killed and 17 injured. I was on the far
side of the airfield at the Squadron dispersal while this took
place and saw it all. I believe it was a Ju 88 that bombed us,
but we all thought it was a Blenheim of No 25 Squadron
approaching to land.

One morning in March, I had finished the daily inspection
that I had been detailed to carry out on a Defiant and had
signed for the serviceability of the aircraft's gun and turret on
the Form 700 when the Flight Mechanic Engines came into
the dispersal hut and informed me that one of the new air-
gunners had got two of the guns out of the turret and stripped.
Sure enough, on my investigating, the sergeant air-gunner had
the guns all in pieces on a waterproof cockpit cover on the
grass. He was not only wrong in interfering with the guns or
mechanism of the turret after I had signed for the serviceability
of them, but he was assembling them wrongly. Of course
there was a hell of a row and I had to report him. There wasn't
an inquiry as such but I believe he had a rocket off the C.O,
and I had an apology from the sergeant. I felt sorry for him,
he was younger than me but I dread to think what would have
happened that night had he tried to fire those guns while in
some action.

March was a poor month for the Squadron regarding any
success against the enemy, although we had aircraft in the air
most nights. I did quite a bit of flying myself during the
daytime when there was a Defiant being test-flown. I took
the place of any air-gunner that didn't want to fly. I enjoyed
the hours. It was a glorious sunny afternoon and I remember

the pilot telling me on the intercom that we could see both the Irish Sea and the North Sea from our height by looking right and then looking left. At that height we were breathing oxygen. I didn't know our height as there was no altimeter in the gun turrets.

The night of April 8th/9th proved to be very rewarding for No 151 Squadron when we were to claim three of the *Luftwaffe* destroyed, two He 111's to Pilot Officer Stevens in his Hurricane and a third to a Defiant. Again on the night of April 9th/10th saw Pilot Officer Stevens for the third time account for two of the *Luftwaffe* in one night, this time a Ju 88 and a He 111. Stevens completed his score for April by shooting down a He 111 on the night of April 19th/20th.

To refer back to our nights out in Stamford, I recall one Saturday night when a crowd of us from No 151 Squadron tried kidnapping a mechanical piano from one of the town centre pubs. I have no idea what we intended to do with the piano had we got in into the street, but fortunately the landlord intervened while it was still only halfway through the front door; I suppose the more sober of us were pleased we got away with just replacing it in the bar. I suppose that after my return from Wolverhampton, and for the remainder of my time with No 151 Squadron, I sort of broke loose and perhaps drank too much and did things I perhaps would normally never have even thought of doing.

Early in April, there was a call for volunteers to teach gun armament at No 3 Ground Armament School (GAS) at RAF Stormy Down in South Wales. This meant promotion to Junior

N.C.O (corporal) on taking up the duties. Never having really been happy on No 151 Squadron after the change to Defiants, I volunteered, I could already see the two stripes on my sleeve!

My posting came through, I was to report to Stormy Down on April 22nd, and with a little wangling, I managed to get a quick station clearance and left Wittering on the afternoon of 21st. I had my Austin to travel in. How did I get the petrol? Well, with friends among the Flight Mechanics and Riggers I had two four gallon cans of Chore Horse petrol hidden behind the front seats and under my overcoat and kit bag plus a full five gallon tank of the same. I left the camp as though I was going out for the evening and was lucky not to have the car searched!

The Parade Square at No 1 RTW, RAF Uxbridge, 1930-40.

No 1 Squad, 'J' Flight, No 1 RTW, Uxbridge, 1938.

'Doiren' Barrack Block, 'J' Flight, No 1 RTW, Uxbridge.

A/C 2 Fred Roberts at No 1 AAS, RAF Manby, March 1939.

*A/C 2 John Andrews
at No 1 AAS, RAF
Manby, March 1939.*

*No 19 Squadron Hangar, RAf Duxford. The white framed
door leads into the Squadron Armoury.*

NAAFI & Dining Hall, RAF Duxford.

No 19 Squadron Barrack Block, RAF Duxford.

No 19 Squadron Armourers & Assistants at Dispersal, RAF Catterick, 1939.

Spitfire Mk Is of 19 Squadron at RAF Duxford in May 1939, 19 Squadron Hangar in background. Note the two-bladed Watts propeller.

Left: 19 Squadron Armourers & Assistants at Dispersal, RAF Hornchurch, at the time of Dunkirk, May/June 1940; from left: Bailey, Roberts, Stanley & Marshall.

19 Squadron Armourers at RAF Fowlmere, July 1940; from left: Marshall, Stanley, Bailey.

19 Squadron's pilots at Fowlmere, July 1940; from left: S/L Lane, Sgt Potter, Sgt Jennings, F/S Unwin, P/O Aeberhardt, F/S Steere, F/O Brinsden, F/L Lawson, F/O Haines, P/O Vokes, F/L Clouston & F/O Thomas (Dilip Sarkar Collection).

Brian Lane's Spitfire at Fowlmere in September 1940; Fred Roberts worked on this aircraft. (IWM)

F/S George 'Grumpy' Unwin DFM & his dog, 'Flash'. Fred Roberts worked on Unwin's Spitfire, 'QV-H'. (Dilip Sarkar Collection).

The famous photograph, taken at Fowlmere in September 1940: Fred Roberts the 'anonymous' armourer, the pilot Sergeant 'Jimmy' Jennings. Incredibly, Fred had not seen this photograph until publication of Dilip Sarkar's first book, 'Spitfire Squadron', in 1990.

Fred & Mary Roberts, both aged 21.

Fred's treasured souvenir of 19 Squadron days, the propeller tip from the Spitfire in which P/O Trenchard lost his life.

*No 19 Squadron Armourers
at Fowlmere, August 1940.*

*Cpls Roberts &
MacDonald relaxing
at No 9 ITW, RAF
Stratford-upon-Avon,
August 1941.*

*Cpls Whitby & MacDonald at
Stratford, 1941.*

*On the River Avon, June
1942; from left: Cpls
Baker, Roberts & Whitby,
of No 9 ITW.*

Imperial Forces Transit Camp, Polsmoor, Cape Town, October 1942. Taken from the Constancia Mountains.

Cpl Roberts after a day's work, No 320 MU, RAF Drigh Road, Karachi, India, early 1943.

Fred relaxing at the RE Bomb Disposal School, Poona, 1943.

The 'Plumber's Arms', Nos 301 & 320 MU, RAF Drigh Road, Karachi, Christmas 1943.

Home from home: in bar of the 'Plumber's Arms'.

Fred (centre) at the Chakrata Rest Camp, Himalayas, 1944.

*All Armourers from Block 34, No 352 MU, Phaphamau,
India, September 1944.*

Again, all Armourers from Block 34, No 352 MU, Phaphamau, India, September 1944.

Cpls Bert Clinton, Allan Galton & Fred Roberts, No 352 MU, Phaphamau, India, 1944.

Fred Roberts and beloved Spitfire at St James's Park, London, July 2005.

Wing Commander Bernard 'Jimmy' Jennings & Fred Roberts, both pictured in the famous Fowlmere photograph, reunited by Dilip Sarkar at the launch of his second book, Great Malvern, 1992; by coincidence the Spitfire Mk XVI was even painted to represent QV-I, the 19 Squadron Spitfire they were photographed with in 1940!

Ernie French, Fred Roberts & John Milne, all ex-19 Squadron 1940, IWM Duxford Air Show, September 2000.

Fred Roberts, left, pictured with S/L 'Stapme' Stapleton DFC (603 Sqn) & Wing Commander George Unwin DSO DFM, Brooklands Museum, May 2000.

Chapter Eleven

STORMY DOWN

No 3 Ground Armament School

I turned left outside the main gates at Wittering, heading for Stamford, but before I got to the airfield boundary I stopped and had one last nostalgic look over the fence at the Beaufighters and Defiants around the dispersal area, and at the hangars in the distance and wondered what my new destination would have in store for me. I hoped that this wasn't to be my finish with aircraft.

I drove as far as Kettering where I encountered an army corporal. He was hitchhiking to his Royal Engineer's Depot at Ashchurch in Gloucestershire. He was lucky as this was on my route to South Wales. It was also fortunate for me that he could drive, because by the time we reached Warwick it was dark and we drove through thick fog from there to Ashchurch. It was a relief to have someone to share the driving with and besides he knew the road.

By the time we reached Ashchurch it was near 2300 hrs and I was knackered. I couldn't have driven any further. I begged a cold supper and a mug of tea from the Sergeant of the Guard at the camp. I was woken at 0500 hrs by one of the sentries and told there was a cooked breakfast waiting for me at the Guard Room. There I was told to eat it up, have a quick wash and shave and beat it before the Military Police came on duty at 0600 hrs. I believe all this kindness was a reward for me giving their corporal a lift the previous evening.

On my arrival at RAF Stormy Down, I was directed to No 3 GAS Orderly Room. From there I was conducted to the living quarters and a wooden hut that was to be my new home, shared by some of the permanent staff including the other instructors. There I was introduced to LAC Husbands (Curly) who like me was a new arrival and a potential instructor. His previous posting had been a Coastal Command Squadron at RAF Aldergrove in Northern Ireland and, again like me, he was a pre-war armourer and Manby-trained. We were to become close friends. We were to find out that evening, when all the other occupants were present, that we were the only instructors that had any squadron experience and were the only regular airmen in the hut.

There was also an Air Gunnery School at Stormy Down, but No 3 GAS was commanded by Squadron Leader Whiting, known by all pre-war Eastchurch-trained Armourers as 'The Fish'. At Eastchurch I believe he was an N.C.O and was hated for his treatment of those under training there. His reputation was well spread throughout the RAF armament fraternity.

The first couple of weeks we were there we sat in on lectures, to quote 'The Fish', 'to listen and learn' before we were 'let loose' on a class of our own. We took a few test lectures, each with an audience of other instructors and the C.O, and were given feedback afterwards.

Neither Curly or myself settled into the routine at No 3 GAS. 'The Fish' was too fond of 'Bull' and we had been used to Squadron routine. The spit and polish and kit inspections, plus the Saturday afternoon drill sessions on the grass of the airfield, didn't go down at all well when we could see all the Air Gunnery School staff and pupils, and the SHQ staff, off duty.

Curly and I went everywhere together. We made the occasional visit to my parents in Neath. We couldn't use the Austin a lot because I only had the five-gallon a month petrol allowance plus a few extra coupons I managed to scrounge through connections in Neath. No Chores Horse petrol at Stormy! We spent a few evenings at the cinema at Kenfig Hill, a small coal mining village. This cinema was hilarious, it had a galvanised steel sheet roof and when it rained, which frequently happened in South Wales, one couldn't hear the sound from the film because of the rain rattling on the steel roof! The roof leaked in places so it was convenient that one could move ones chair (not seat) to a drier spot!

Porthcawl, a seaside resort was quite near to Stormy but we never felt any inclination to visit. Most of our time out of camp we either hitchhiked or took a bus, mostly to Bridgend. We made quite a few friendships (casual) among the Bridgend female fraternity. There were a lot of girls there, local and those that had been directed to war work at the nearby explosive factory and I could say they were dynamite!

Our stay at Stormy wasn't to be of long duration. Before we were given our promotion and allowed to teach we were summoned into the presence of Squadron Leader Whiting who informed us that we weren't suitable for his school. He considered that we were scruffy in uniform and undisciplined and too friendly with the pupils. But he did say that he couldn't fault our knowledge of armament or our ability to teach, but we would never reach his standard of smartness. We began to think that he hadn't been told there was a war on.

We tried to explain that it wasn't possible to keep two suits of best blue uniforms on squadron and he wouldn't believe that working overalls disappeared when the war started. He had no experience of living rough in tents and Nissen huts, or ever heard of people working on aircraft in grease and oil with no protective clothing. In fact I could still smell the anti-freeze paste on my working uniform, the paste we smeared on the aircraft wings to prevent icing when night flying. He could only see that Curly and I wouldn't fit his idea of what an instructor should be and told us that he would be filling the posts with the best of the current new trainees when they passed their final examinations. He also told us that we wouldn't be promoted and that he had applied to have us returned to active squadrons. I will say that my short stay at No 3 GAS wasn't without its reward because I found my newly acquired teaching knowledge invaluable in my new posting.

It was late May when Curly and I were informed we were posted to No 9 Initial Training Wing (ITW) at Stratford upon Avon. I had nothing like the amount of petrol to drive the Austin there so I had to leave it with my parents at Neath. My Mother was quick to sell it for me but I am still waiting for the money!

Chapter Twelve

STRATFORD-UPON-AVON

No 9 Initial Training Wing

April 21st, 1941, saw Curly Husbands and me moving to Stratford-upon-Avon. This time it was a train ride from Bridgend, changing trains at Cardiff. I remember the train from Cardiff was two diesel rail cars coupled together, a novelty then but the forerunner of the modern sprinter trains. We arrived at Stratford mid-afternoon. Our instructions were to report to the Arden Hotel, the railway staff of Stratford informed us that this was in Waterside, at the far end of the town and facing the Shakespeare Memorial Theatre.

We quickly found our way there to be greeted with the news that No 9 ITW was a new unit, yet to be formed, and that No 9 Receiving Wing was the unit in residence at that time. The Arden and adjacent Udimore Hotel contained the headquarters of No 9 ITW Receiving Wing and was to be the headquarters of No 9 ITW. We were introduced to a Corporal Smith, who had arrived a few hours before us. He was to be a colleague and also an armourer. He had learned that No 9 ITW was to be an initial training unit for aircrew and we were to be armament instructors (so much for our postings back to squadrons). We were the first of the armament staff to be posted there but were told that there were a few Drill Instructor Corporals and one Leading Aircraftman Wireless Operator Instructor who had arrived earlier that day.

After giving all our details at the Orderly Room, the three of us were conducted to the Shakespeare Hotel where we were given a meal and told that it was the dining room for permanent staff. From the Shakespeare Hotel we were taken back to the Arden Hotel where we picked up our kitbags and were then taken to the Stratford Hotel in Gregory's Road. This was to be our home for the unforeseeable future. The hotel had been commandeered by the RAF but at that time had just a few personnel billeted there, so we had the freedom to choose a room of our liking. We found a room containing three beds and lockers and a wash hand basin and with a view over the rooftops of the town. We also had a bathroom and toilet adjacent to the room. There was an abundance of hot water and radiator heating if we needed it. The boilers were controlled and maintained by a civilian gentleman. This was a luxury, except we had to walk perhaps a mile for breakfast in the morning.

I think we spent that first evening in one of the local pubs talking about our respective past couple of years. Corporal Smith, 'Ginger' as he became known to all of us, was also a Manby-trained armourer but senior to us. He had been on a bomber squadron in Yorkshire prior to volunteering for this posting; he was a Yorkshire man himself, being from Pontefract.

After breakfast the next day, we again reported to the orderly room at the Arden Hotel. Being early arrivals for No 9 ITW and the unit not having been formed, no one there knew what to do with us. We suggested that we should leave but there was no one with the authority to give permission for this.

Eventually we were sent to the Avonside Hotel to do a bit of gardening. There under the guidance of an old gentleman, the gardener, we were given a plot of ground to 'Dig' (Digging for Victory). We three managed to spread this over the best part of a week, interspersed with tea breaks in a church canteen across the road from the garden and run by some local young ladies from the nearby Holy Trinity Church. It was a hot sunny week and I think we all enjoyed our gardening. It was different and certainly loosened up those muscles that had stiffened in us over the previous few weeks. Stripped to the waist it also gave us a beautiful sun tan.

The following week saw the arrival of Flight Lieutenant Leslie Ames, the Kent and England cricketer, who was to be the Armament and Signals Officer. Also over the next two weeks, the remainder of the armament staff arrived. These were:

Sergeant Noad	Senior Armament NCO
Corporal Johnston	Instructor
LAC (Mac) MacDonald	Instructor
LAC (Lofty) Whitby	Instructor
LAC (Johnny) Travis	Instructor
LAC (Jock) Munro	Instructor

Including us three, this made a total of eight instructors and we were all to teach armament to the air crew cadets under training.

Sergeant Noad was accommodated in the Shakespeare Hotel, but the remainder of the lads were along with us three in the Stratford. We were kept busy until the opening of No 9 ITW on June 14th, 1941, sorting out classrooms, four rooms in the Grove House, an ex-preparatory school opposite the local cinema. This is where Curly, Mac, Ginger and I were to instruct, and four classrooms in the Firs Hotel in Rother Street, where Johnny, Lofty, Jock and Johnston were to teach. We had to set up tables and forms, plan instruction schedules, timetables were set by Headquarters, then we had to sort out and clean all the Vickers K guns, Browning guns and revolvers that were to be used for instructional purposes.

The ITW training itinerary also consisted of signalling instructions by Morse Key and Aldis Lamp, which were taught by wireless operator personnel. Navigation was taught by ex-school teachers holding honorary commissions in the RAF. The cadets also participated in the normal activities run by Drill and Physical Training N.C.Os.

Most of the big hotels in Stratford had been commandeered by the RAF and the aircrew cadets were to be accommodated in them throughout the town along with their respective drill instructors. These cadets were at first all new recruits to the armed forces but later were to include re-musterings from RAF ground staff and, by a large majority, transfers from army regiments.

On June 14th, 1941, the unit was officially launched under the command of Wing Commander Hays, an ex- Royal Flying Corps pilot and the millionaire owner of Hays Wharf and Cartage Company.

We were all soon settled in our hotels and classrooms and I believe were proving to be quite successful in teaching armament to all those potential aircrew, most of whom had never before seen a machine-gun. Our only failure was Johnston, who had such a broad southern Irish accent that the cadets had difficulty understanding what he was talking about. Our duties never consisted of more than three two-hour lectures a day. On a rare day perhaps only one lecture and there was a night duty every 16th night when we took charge of the fire-picket in Grove House. We shared this duty with the wireless instructors. The rest of the time was our own, with every Saturday and Sunday free. We would never have known there was a war on had it not been for the newspapers and the nightly air raids on Midland towns.

For the next few months the weather was beautiful, with nearly every day being hot and sunny, leading to all the armourers, with the exception of Sergeant Noad and Corporal Johnston, learning and participating in the relaxing hobbies of rowing, canoeing and punting on the River Avon. None of us had any previous experience of this activity so we had to learn from scratch. We were lucky not to have any accidents, such as falling off the back of the put or tipping up the boat or canoe. The opportunity of a free afternoon or evening on the river was a great puller with the local and visiting lassies. I think the fare was something like a shilling, or 5p, for an hour's hire of the craft at forces' rate; we had to leave our gas respirators with the boat owners as a guarantee of the safe return of the craft and payment for hire.

We used to await the arrival of the trains from Birmingham, Leamington and Coventry at the GWR Railway Station on Sunday mornings for the influx of young ladies, and we could select our companion of the day. This wasn't at all difficult, it wasn't Shakespeare they came to Stratford to see!

There was also cricket to watch if one was interested, on evenings or Saturdays on the recreation ground, and there was both the local cinema and Shakespeare Memorial Theatre to visit if one was so inclined. During the summer season, only Shakespeare's plays were performed at the theatre.

In September, we armourers and the wireless operators were moved from the Stratford Hotel to a private but commandeered house in Alcester Road. This move coincided with all the LAC armourers being promoted to corporal. This was the promotion that Curly and I had been promised back in April at Stormy Down, the promotion to be dated from September 1st, 1941. This time Mac moved into a bedroom with we three originals, but with this move we lost all our luxurious living quarters. We were overcrowded and had only one toilet and bathroom between 16 of us, but it was much better than tents in the Western Desert!

It was lectures and lectures right through the months. As autumn came upon us the visitors stopped coming at weekends and our night life became perhaps twice weekly visits to the cinema, or a pint of beer and a game of darts in the Seven Stars public house.

I should mention that throughout the summer months we saw very little of Flight Lieutenant Ames, he was away playing cricket for the Home Counties Eleven. It was Sergeant Noad who ran the Armament Section.

It was during the autumn that rifle firing was introduced into the curriculum. We took over the ex-Territorial Army rifle range at Bordon Hill, outside the town. We taught rifle firing with .300 P14 calibre rifles, taking two classes of cadets at a time. With two instructors in charge, one instructor taking control of the target area and the other in control of the firing area. The armament staff also had use of the small bore indoor range in the Territorial Hall in the town. This facility we took great advantage of in the cold weather. We had some .22 calibre rifles and a plentiful supply of ammunition supplied at the same time as the P14 rifles. Great rivalry arose among us armourers in competitions held between ourselves. Neither Noad nor Johnston shared any of these activities with the other seven of us.

With the oncoming of colder weather, none of us could spend any of our between-lectures time having a stroll along the riverside or around the town, but we found warmth for a few hours in Burtons Snooker Hall. It became well known that the armament staff could be found there if needed. The Station Warrant Officer, I believe, I started referring to it as Burton's Armoury. Mid-morning tea we took at the Tudor Café, near Grove House.

There was no heating of any kind in our house in Alcester Road and this led to all of us spending as little time there as possible. Neither had we any heating at the start of winter in Grove House. I can remember lecturing with myself and cadets wearing overcoats and gloves. Our colleagues giving lectures in the Firs Hotel were more fortunate. They had centrally heated classrooms, but we survived and eventually we were supplied with paraffin-burning heaters which made conditions a little more comfortable.

During the autumn and winter, there were Saturday night dances in the Conference Hall, a part of the Memorial Theatre, which had been taken over by the RAF and was the unit NAAFI. There were also a variety of non-Shakespeare plays being performed at the Memorial Theatre including Sheridan's 'School for Scandal' and I remember the 1941 Christmas pantomime 'Cinderella' with Ted Ray taking the part of Buttons.

I was due a few days leave. This I took early in December, travelling home to South Wales. I remember collecting chocolate and sweets over the previous few weeks as a Christmas treat for my brother and two sisters. Mac and me had become firm friends by this time and between us had accumulated about twenty bars, which I packed in my case. During the train journey, not thinking, I pushed the case under the seat in the train, the luggage rack being full. On arriving home I found the under seat steam heating pipes had melted the chocolate. What a mess! On resetting, the chocolate had assumed unrecognisable shapes and was all stuck to the paper wrapping. There was no foil wrapping during the war years but I was assured by my mother that it was all enjoyed on Christmas Day.

Also, just before Christmas, Flight Lieutenant Ames turned up at Grove House with a large Christmas cake baked by Mrs Ames and a nine gallon barrel of Flowers best bitter for us as a thank you for all the good work carried out in his absence the previous months.

A number of us living in Alcester Road were invited to a Christmas party with the female staff of Stratford-upon-Avon General Hospital. I think three of us accepted the invitation, some of the lads had already made arrangements to spend leave at their homes. I know Ginger Smith and Mac went with me and we were also invited to a New Year's Eve party, again with the hospital female staff. We all had a really enjoyable time at both these events with all the food and more than one could expect under war-time rationing, and there was plenty of drink if one so desired.

It was at the first party that I was introduced to Mary Rogers, a very good looking and attractive young lady. I was immediately attracted by her friendliness and bubbling humour and I knew that this was the girl I wanted to be with. Edna Mold and I had been perhaps more than just good friends for two years, but I never had the feeling with her that I felt this time with Mary. We formed a friendship that soon grew to a feeling much stronger than anything I had known before. We were soon to be seeing each other on every opportunity, but more of Mary later.

Into 1942 and another year of war gone, but since May 1941 it seemed the war had never happened to me and the others at Stratford. We had no rationing and lived in good billets and dined in the best hotel, the Shakespeare, although the fare was of service quality.

In January 1941, Johnnie Travis and I were detailed to instruct the members of the local police division in rifle firing at Bordon Hill rifle range. The police were only to be allowed five rounds of ammunition per man per occasion. This didn't make a policeman's visit to the range really worthwhile, so by adjusting the ammunition records we managed about 20 rounds per policeman per occasion and were suitably rewarded with two or perhaps three large packets of cigarettes each on each visit. We were transported to and from the range by the police.

It was early in 1942 that we stopped teaching the Vickers K gun and started teaching the 20 mm Hispano Cannon. This was the same gun that I had worked on during my time with No 19 Squadron. This gave me an advantage over the other armourers as I was the only one who had previously worked on the cannon. Also at this time the unit was allocated two-double barrelled 12-bore shot guns, with ammunition and a clay pigeon trap, the machine for throwing the clay pigeon into the air. Permission was granted through our headquarters to allow us to experiment with equipment on the seven meadows adjacent to the River Avon and the LMS Railway Station at Stratford.

Four or perhaps, five of us transported all the necessary equipment to the site, the clay pigeon trap being bolted to a large baulk of timber. This was to give us some experience before being let loose with the cadets. After a few trial throws with the trap but no firing, we started to fire at the clays. None of us had ever had any experience of firing shot guns before. The guns were kicking heavily and I'm afraid we were all well off the mark in our aiming. We were also throwing the clays in the wrong direction, that is towards the railway station and we soon had a hurried visit from the Station Master who came running, shouting and waving his arms, to tell us we were endangering his passengers and staff on the station platform as we were peppering the station with 12-bore shot! That was the first and only time 12-bore shooting took place at No 9 ITW while I was there.

February saw me receiving a posting to RAF Evanton in Scotland on an Air Gunnery Course, a course I neither applied for or wanted. Sometime early in 1940 when air gunners were in short supply, an Air Ministry instruction was issued that some armourers were to be sent on air gunnery courses. It was a case of you, you and you, and this was the result of that Air Ministry instruction. I was told when the posting came through that it was now a voluntary posting, so I quickly declined and it was cancelled.

About this time, Curly Husbands and Jock Munro were posted to RAF Reykjavik in Iceland. Jock had only a few days before his posting arrived back from leave with the exciting news that his wife had presented him with a baby son after many years of marriage, so it was quite upsetting for him having only had those few days with his new family. Once again, the fortunes of war.

The replacement instructors were two new Corporals, Baker, who was immediately dubbed 'Spud', and Brown, who because of his size became known as 'Tubby'. They came together, straight from a Gun Armament School with no practical experience of any kind. Promotion came so easily to new service entries in 1942, but we had had to work hard for our promotion. About six months previously, Brown was a postman in Bristol and Baker was a representative for a worldwide stationery firm; ironically he was also a member of the governing body of the Kent County Cricket Club where our Armament Officer Leslie Ames was a professional player, so their status was reversed and it was Baker who had to do the Siring and Saluting. Again the fortunes of war.

By this time, Mary and I were seeing each other on every opportunity. I was spending most evening with her and if she happened to be on duty I was always invited into the staff sitting room to wait until her duty finished at 2000 hrs. I was often given a cooked supper from the Hospital Kitchen, which was a bonus. My life might have seemed boring at this time, what with all the air activity with fighter squadrons in the South and all the bomber squadron activities in the Eastern Counties airfields, but I must be honest and say that although many times I missed squadron life, and felt like volunteering to return to fighters, by this time I had formed so great a love for Mary that I wouldn't have done anything to precipitate a move from Stratford. I know she returned that love.

The cadets that were arriving at No 9 ITW these first few months of 1942 were mostly volunteers from army regiments, with a sprinkling of re-musterings from the RAF. These ex-soldiers were already versed in some form of armament, which made our teaching a lot easier. As a result a lot of humour crept into the classrooms. Lectures and lectures, the cadets came in their hundreds, preparing for the future bombing onslaught on Germany in the coming years. Stratford's streets were nothing but a massive parade ground with marching airmen, and we were No 9 ITW!

Early April, we were warned of an impending visit by some unknown high-ranking personage from the Air Ministry. Having seen such dignitaries as Air Chief Marshal, Sir Hugh Dowding and Air Vice-Marshal Sir Trafford Leigh-Mallory at Duxford in 1940, I didn't attach much importance to this, but on April 12th, we were ordered to wear our best blue uniforms on the following day. One of the squadrons of cadets and a squadron of WAAFs were paraded for inspection by the visitors on the morning in question. This was held on Waterside, in front of the Unit Headquarters, the Arden Hotel. We were instructed to keep out of sight, or at least keep our heads down in our classrooms.

It was early in the afternoon while instructing a class on 20 mm cannon that there was a knock on the classroom door and the Station Warrant Officer entered with a barked order, "Attention". A party of officers walked into the room. These included our C.O, Wing Commander Hays, and to my surprise, His Royal Highness, Air Commodore, The Duke of Kent, and, more to my surprise, he immediately put us all at ease by saying, "Please sit down. Corporal, carry on." The party remained about 10 minutes although it seemed an hour. The Duke did ask a couple of questions about the cannon during his stay and seemed pleased with the answers I gave him. It is nice to be ale to say, with tongue in cheek, that I lectured royalty. It was just a few months later in August that we heard, with sadness, that the Duke of Kent had been killed in a flying accident. The Sunderland flying boat in which he was travelling crashed in a remote part of Scotland, while en route to Iceland; there was only one survivor.

I should have mentioned previously that there was always a celebration amongst cadets the evening before leaving No 9 ITW. The high spot of these celebration was the ducking of the statue of 'Prince Hal', a Shakespearean character, into the canal basin in front of the Memorial Theatre, and the fancy dressing up of the statue of Shakespeare himself, usually finishing with painting him a red nose. The local police tried hard to prevent this happening, but, despite knowing the dates of courses passing out, never succeeded in stopping it happening.

The warmer weather was with us again and we were able to take up our boating activities on the river. This time I was more fortunate as I had the company of Mary and being a member of the Stratford hospital staff she had the use of the hospital boat. This gave the two of us many an hour of pleasurable free boating on Mary's evening off duty. By this time we were both certain of our feelings for each other. I had been taken to her home at Temple Grafton, a village six miles from Stratford and introduced to her parents. I had already met her sister who lived and worked in Stratford.

There seemed to be no end to the volunteers for aircrew, as one squadron passed out and moved onto flying training there was another to take their place. I don't know how many ITWs there were altogether, but we were kept busy.

The month of May arrived and with Spring in the air, I thought the time propitious and proposed to Mary. Despite us knowing each other for just a few months I knew I was making the right choice. I don't think there was any hesitation in her answer and I soon bought the ring and we became officially engaged; after 62 years of marriage I know that I made the right decision. Of course there was the sort of ragging that went with these occasions. There were a few celebration pints in the Seven Stars pub and the "you'll regret it" from Whitby, Baker and Brown, all of whom were married men.

The moths passed all too quickly and in July, Mary and I spent a week together at Watchet in Somerset. The weather was glorious and we had long walks, some sea bathing and in the evenings, a few drinks in one or other of the local inns. We stayed bed and breakfast and evening meals with a family that took boarders during the summer months. It was during this holiday that we decided to marry in September, and after announcing the news to her parents on our arriving back at Stratford, we set in motion all the arrangements, such as having the banns called at Temple Grafton Church, where we were to be married, and at Stratford-upon-Avon Holy Trinity Church, which was the unit church.

Everything was going well. Potential aircrew were arriving and departing regularly. We were enjoying our off-duty times on the river and in other pursuits. We were always busy. Mary and I had the banns called for the first time in our respective churches on Sunday, August 9th, 1942, but then the bomb exploded. On Saturday, August 15th, I was called to the Orderly Room at the Arden Hotel and told I was posted overseas, and that I was to leave for RAF Wilmslow in Cheshire on Monday August 17th. I was shattered by the news. I didn't know what to do first, whether to get my clearance from No 9 ITW or find Mary and break the news to her. Fortunately I started the round of clearance signatures and whilst with the Station Adjutant, I mentioned that I had had the banns called the previous Sunday and was upset with the posting at that time. He asked me if I still wanted to marry and on my assuring him he made a few telephone calls and arranged for the posting to be delayed until Tuesday, August 18th. Then through Canon Prentice, the Vicar at Holy Trinity Church, he arranged for me to collect a special licence to marry from the Diocese Office at Coventry on the morning of August 17th. After this I had to find Mary at the hospital and explain everything so that she could make arrangements at Temple Grafton with the Vicar to have the wedding brought forward from September to the afternoon of August 17th, and also to make other arrangements with her parents.

At Coventry, I found a long queue of people waiting at the bus station. I needed to get back to Stratford in time for the wedding. I had to go to the front of the queue, Special Wedding Licence in my hand and beg of the bus conductor and waiting passengers to allow me to jump the queue. Everyone light heartedly and jokingly pushed me onto the bus. I thought at one stage they were going to have a whip round for a wedding present for me! I arrived at Stratford and met up with my best mate, Mac, who had arranged a day off and who was to be my Best Man. He had borrowed Whitby's bicycle and had also procured another for me from somewhere and we cycled to Temple Grafton. Yes! Cycled to my wedding, perhaps unusual but I can say there was a war on. Everything was so rushed but turned out successfully in the end; we were married with little fuss at 1500 hrs that Monday.

Tuesday, August 18th, and back to Stratford, cycling again, this time with Mary, now my wife, to pick up my Movement Orders and to thank the Adjutant and others for everything, and to collect my kit. Then, with a tearful farewell for Mary and myself at the railway station, it was a train to Wilmslow.

Chapter Thirteen

TROOPSHIPS TO INDIA

I remember very little of RAF Wilmslow. I know the transit camp was tented with wooden dining hall and stores and to be a depressing and not very welcoming place. The permanent Senior N.C.Os there treated us all as less than numbers, I believe, men to be got rid of as soon as possible, altogether not the sort of treatment to give people going abroad for years, or perhaps not to return at all, not the kind of air force personnel I knew.

There were perhaps a couple of thousand of us, junior N.C.Os and airmen billeted in the tents and we were to form Draft No 6918. We weren't given any information about where our ultimate destination was to be. Things like that weren't possible in wartime. We spent the first few days at Wilmslow exchanging clothing, handing in one suit of blue and a pair of boots in exchange for a khaki tunic, trousers, shorts, shirts, khaki long socks and a pair of shoes plus one pith helmet. The tunic and shorts were all ill-fitting, we all looked a right mob of goons. We were also subjected to inoculations and vaccinations of all kinds and had to submit to a lot of documentation.

Come Saturday morning, August 22nd, we were told that any of us that had a necessary need to return home and lived within a reasonable distance of Wilmslow could have a pass out until

2359 hrs the following Monday, August 24th. Only that morning I had received a letter from Mary, on Stratford-upon-Avon Hospital headed writing paper, so hoping for the best I presented it to the officer giving out and signing Form 295s, telling him my wife was in hospital, which was true. He didn't read the letter but just gave me the Form 295 to fill in and then signed it, but the forms were then handed over to the permanent staff senior N.C.O to hand out to us after duty hours.

After dinner at 1200 hrs, when there were no officers to take a complaint to, we were informed by the Permanent Staff N.C.Os that we could all either play 'Housey Housey' (bingo) or go on a route march in the surrounding district, but we would not be given our passes until 1700 hrs. This was a fiddle to take money off us, the larger portion of that money going into the N.C.Os' pockets. The majority of us chose to go on the route march, thereby ensuring that some of those N.C.Os suffered with us.

This made all of us going south from Wilmslow unable to get a train until about 1900 hrs. By the time we got to the suburbs of Birmingham there was an air raid warning in being. This led to a further delay of another two hours. I arrived in Birmingham to find the last train to Stratford-upon-Avon had gone, but I did manage to get a trolleybus to Hall Green, then walked the remainder of the way, some 24 miles, arriving at the hospital at about 0400 hrs on the Sunday morning. The night staff at the hospital informed me that Mary was asleep after waiting up late, expecting me (I had phoned from Wilmslow Station), but I wouldn't let them wake her. So they found me a bed in a single ward where I slept soundly until Mary woke me at about 0800 hrs.

We had a quick breakfast then Mary borrowed a bike for me from, I think, one of the hospital porters, then we cycled to her home at Temple Grafton. The next 24 hours flew by. We had so much to talk about. We both knew that I would not be home again for at least three years. I could tell her that I was either going to the Middle or the Far East, that I could guess at because we had been issued with the khaki drill and pith helmet. After another tearful farewell on Stratford Station Monday morning, it was back to Wilmslow.

A few more days and on August 27th, we were transported to Bootle and thence by tramcar to the Pier Headquarters at Liverpool, where we embarked on HM Troopship D 19, formerly the Royal Mail Liner *RMS Andes*. Our draft was accommodated on F deck, and in which I believe was the ship's ballroom when in its peace time role. There were about 4,000 Navy and RAF personnel, perhaps more by the time we sailed on August 28th, accompanied by another troop ship, *Orcades*, which had been berthed behind us at Liverpool.

We met up with a lot of other ships in the next 24 hours, that we were told had sailed from Glasgow and together we formed a large convoy. I remember having quite an unhappy first couple of days, suffering sea sickness along with some thousand more. We eventually arrived in Freetown in East Africa, where we anchored for three days whilst the ship took on fresh water. I remember the lads throwing coins into the water there and the bumboat boys diving for them. Most of our time on board ship was spent playing cards and eating four good meals a day of food that would only have been found in England before the war, and of a standard that most of us had never known previously. It was a few days after leaving Freetown that I was tempted to buy a card in the Housey Housey school that was held on deck twice daily. I had never been tempted to place a bet before and with beginners luck I won £24. This was a lot of money in 1942 and proved a real bonus in the future weeks. We were only paid 10/- (50p) per week while in transit.

We crossed the Equator soon after leaving Freetown and all the celebrations associated with crossing the line were carried out. King Neptune came aboard, but on this occasion only a few of the RAF and RN officers and the Wren officers and a few RN ratings were initiated into his court and afterwards presented with a certificate, acknowledging the event.

We were all awakened at dawn on September 25th, by the ships tannoy system, with the news that Table Mountain at Cape Town was in view on the port side of the ship, with the sun rising behind it. There was a mad scramble by all on board to see this and it was something I will always remember. It was a wonderful sight and I was told afterwards by the Cape residents that what we saw was a rarity as the table top was most mornings shrouded in mist or cloud like a table cloth.

Soon after docking we were given passes, allowing us ashore from 1600 hrs until 2359 hrs. I spent the intervening hour to 1600 hrs at the ship's side, watching all the comings and going on the dockside, everything was so new and in most cases, strange to me. What surprised me most, I think, was to see lorries arriving which were loaded with oranges and tipping them over the quay into the sea. This, we were told, was because there was no room on the ships to export them. What would the children at home have given for them? We were to find out how much surplus fruit of all kinds there was in the next few weeks, and it was given to us free.

By this time I had made friends with another Armament N.C.O, Corporal Percy Hemmings who originated from Swindon. We spent that evening and the next afternoon and evening exploring Cape Town. We were made welcome everywhere but cautioned against going into certain suburbs of the city where we were likely to be set upon by Broederbond Africaners who were anti-British. September 27th our draft was disembarked and we were taken by train to the Imperial Forces Transit Camp at Retreat, Pollsmoor. This was about 14 miles from Cape Town and was on the Cape Town to Muizenberg and Simonstown road. The other draft of airmen that was on board the RMS *Andes* was disembarked before us and taken by train across South Africa to Durban. There was talk that they were destined for the Middle East. We were also told by the crew of the Andes that the ship was returning to England via New York, transporting American servicemen to England, so much for security!

We were billeted in a tented camp and it was rough, but we were told that it was only temporary. During the first few days at Retreat, I would think 90% of us were to suffer diarrhoea. This was no doubt due to the amount of fruit we were consuming, a diet we were not used to. We were in tents for perhaps five days, then transferred to a brand new hutted camp nearby. We armourers were allocated Hut 29 in Block 6.

We had a very easy life while at Retreat. We had breakfast at 0800 hrs and paraded at 0900 hrs. some mornings we were taken on a short route march. It depended on which officer took the parade. Otherwise we had no duties. We were allowed out of the camp from 1330 hrs until 0130 hrs the following morning. We found that on making our way to the railway station (1/- {10p} return to Cape Town) that there were scores of cars parked along the main Cape Town road. The pro-British population had turned out to take us to their homes or to visit the local beauty spots or go the seaside town of Muizenberg. We were given a magnificent welcome and this I understand was given to all British and Commonwealth troops throughout the war years. We were all to make lots of friends during our stay. I believe some of the lads made lasting friendships with the young daughters of families we met.

We were given free tram tickets to travel in the city and suburbs, complimentary cinema tickets and reduced train fares from Retreat to the city and sometimes being taken into the homes of the Cape people. I remember four of us being taken by a family to their home in Sea Point; they had a reinforced glass floor to their lounge that was over the sea and the water being so clear one could see the fish swimming below. We also spent a lot of our time swimming at Muizenberg, which was only a 30 minute walk from the camp. There were shark nets in the sea some yards from the beach to prevent bathers being attacked. We also did a bit of mountain climbing on the Constancia mountains at the back of the camp.

Unfortunately, this was not to last. About November 28th, on the morning parade, we were instructed to pack our kit because

Draft 6918 was leaving after our midday meal. We were taken by train to Cape Town docks and boarded the troopship *Ascania*. This was a cargo/passenger vessel of unknown vintage that had been transporting Italian prisoners of war from Egypt to Mombassa. We were accommodated in tiered bed bunks in the holds, nothing like the accommodation in RMS *Andes*. We left Cape Town in the company of about a dozen other cargo vessels within a few hours of our embarking and a few hours after rounding the Cape Town of Good Hope we sailed into a tropical storm that lasted the whole way to Durban where we arrived five days later. I believe the whole draft suffered from sea sickness during this short voyage. The ship tossed and rolled something terrible, or so it seemed to us landlubbers, the only thing it didn't do was turn turtle! I spent the entire five days and four nights on the open deck, sleeping at night with others under a large tarpaulin sheet and eating very little. The food was horrible anyway and it was a relief to enter the calm waters of Durban Harbour.

One outstanding memory I have of arriving at Durban was to see and hear Perla Siedle Gibson, better known as 'Durban's Lady in White', standing in the rain on the dockside wearing a white raincoat and hat, holding a white umbrella in one hand and singing a welcome song to us through her megaphone (no microphone for her). She sang popular and patriotic songs to us. She was there for all arriving and departing troopships throughout the war.

On disembarking from the *Ascania* we were taken by train to the Imperial Forest Transit Camp at Clarewood. This was about four miles from Durban and near Clarewood racecourse.

Here we didn't have the same kind of welcome from the Durban people as we had at the Cape Town, but Durban did have a lot of excellent Forces' Canteens and Clubs, the Navy Club being very good, but the best of all was the Jewish Club. There we had a welcome equal to the best anywhere in the world.

Durban had a worse reputation than Cape Town for anti-British feeling from the Broederbond Africaners. We were not allowed out of Clarewood Camp unless we were in parties of four or more, and had to stay as such otherwise we would have been arrested by the Military Police. So we spent little time there sightseeing and never stopped after dark, despite being allowed pass from 1400 hrs until 2359 hrs. The weather whilst we were there was mostly misty rain and very humid. I do remember walking through the sugar cane plantations near the camp and sucking the sugar cane that we were given. It was very sweet and there was again an abundance of fresh fruit everywhere.

We left Durban about December 8th on the Union Castle liner *Stirling Castle*, and this time Percy Hemmings and I, and all the other armourers and the rest of Draft 6918, were on 'C' deck, which was deep in the ship. Most of the lads were to sleep in hammocks, some on the floor, but I must admit to pulling rank and claiming the mess table top, but this had one drawback, I had to vacate the table early every morning to allow the lads to have their breakfast. There was no lie in for me, but at least I wasn't bumped or trod on during the night! We had none of the luxuries that we enjoyed on the *Andes*. There was no dining room for us in the lower portions of the ship, all our food had to be carried down several decks from the ships kitchens to where we were accommodated. Although as an N.C.O I was spared this duty, and we were eight men to a mess table, the food which was very good, was carried in tins or on trays.

We also had some other thousands of airmen and soldiers on board who had come direct from England, enjoying just a few days at Durban en route. We sailed from Durban in the company of another troopship and a Royal Navy cruiser, and sailed direct to Bombay, arriving 11 days later.

We were allowed ashore on the afternoon and evening of the day of our arrival at Bombay and that was enough for me. The smell of the place and of the larger portion of the population was overpowering. I was soon back on board ship. But a few of my fellow airmen seemed to have lost their heads and money buying souvenirs, some even bough fake kukri's (Ghurkha knives), for what I don't know.

The next morning Draft 6918 was marched a half mile along the dock to another much smaller ship that, until the Japanese invaded Java, had been a river boat. It was flat bottomed and rolled and rocked even in Bombay Harbour where it was anchored for a few days before we sailed. A lot of the draft was this time allocated to a cabin. It was comfortable but the food was the worst I have ever had. On the days we were anchored in Bombay Harbour, and the days we were sailing to Karachi, we lived on ship's biscuits which were rock hard and contained weevils, and tins of Maconichies stew, plenty of tea to drink but made with condensed milk. Were we glad to see Karachi and get our feet on dry land! At one time we thought we were going to spend Christmas on that ship.

Chapter Fourteen

RAF DRIGH ROAD,
KARACHI, INDIA

Christmas Eve, December 24th, 1942. So much had happened in the previous 12 months that they seem to have been very short. I had met, courted and married the young lady that was to be my life partner, I had made new friends, I had met and spoken to important people, including royalty, and had travelled far and wide.

And now, along with hundreds of other young airmen like myself, I was disembarking from an ex-Japanese river boat onto the dockside at Karachi. A train was waiting and it was a short journey to the Royal Air Force Station at Drigh Road, which was situated on the edge of the Sind Desert and about six miles from the town of Karachi. The camp had its own railway station where we detrained, and from where we were then marched through the main camp to a tented site where we were left to decide for ourselves with whom and which tent we wanted to share. Somewhere during the disembarking and the short train journey I seem to have lost touch with my fellow armourers and finished up in a tent with some electricians and a carpenter. We were six men to a tent and were soon to become good friends.

After a meal of sorts in a large marquee, we were issued with a mosquito net, two blankets, two sheets and a bolster, no biscuits (mattresses) here. Instead we were issued with a Durri, carpet like piece of material to lay on the Charpoy (rope bed) under the blanket. This Durri was also used to roll up one's bedding in while moving about India on postings, etc. We were then left to our own devices and to settle in, in our new surroundings with the instructions that we were to parade the next morning after breakfast outside the dining marquee.

Christmas morning and on parade we were addressed by the Station Commander, Group Captain Rutter. We were told that our draft was unexpected until a few hours before arrival and as such there wasn't sufficient Christmas fare to give us what he, the C.O, would have liked, but the cooks would do their best. I remember that we had a good Christmas dinner, including tinned pudding and custard, that I feel sure had rum in it, but our 'turkey' that day was corned beef. The main camp had Guinea Fowl, but they hadn't enough to share with our hungry mob.

We were also informed that there was no NAAFI in India. All the military canteens were run by a contractor by the name of Waza Ali and were staffed only by those of the Islamic faith.

For washing and bathing purposes, we were allowed one bowl of water every morning. The bowls were kept in the ablution blocks. First, the water was used to clean our teeth, then to wash, finally to pour the remainder over oneself as a sort of quick shower bath, but the showers were only turned on daily between 1600 hrs and 1700 hrs, so one had to be quick.

Boxing Day morning, December 26th, we were all paraded and issued with extra pairs of short trousers and blue flannel short working shirts. After this parade, we armourers were told that we were part of the newly formed No 320 Maintenance Unit (MU). Percy Hemmings and I were placed in charge of the Assembly Flight under a Flight Sergeant Fitter Armourer, an Irishman whose name I have forgotten, and we had working under us a dozen or so armourers and some Ghurkha labourers.

Our work was to take part in the assembly of Hawker Hurricane Mk IIA, IIB and IIC aircraft that were arriving from England in wooden crates. We also assisted in the assembly of Vultee Vengeance dive-bombers that were arriving crated from the USA.

The Hurricane guns and cannons were packed in separate wooden boxes inside the aircraft crates, four Browning guns or two Hispano cannons to a box. After removal of the guns or cannons, the boxes were broken up and burnt under a large steel vat of water. This was used to boil the cannons to remove the thick grease that covered them to protect them from corrosion. The Browning guns were washed in petrol to remove the grease. This work was carried out by the Ghurkhas under the supervision of one of our LAC Armourers. After de-greasing the guns and cannons were stripped examined and re-assembled by the armourers and then installed in the Hurricanes.

The armament on the Vultee Vengeance was unprotected by grease, so all that was necessary was a thorough examination, and then installation of the rear guns. The Vengeance armament consisted of four Browning's, two in each wing firing forward, and two Browning .303 calibre guns in the rear cockpit on a swivel mounting. Later versions of the aircraft had only a single browning .50 calibre gun in the rear cockpit. The aircraft was also equipped to carry bombs on internal racks in the fuselage and had an external bomb rack under each wing. These external bomb racks we removed and secured to the internal racks in the bomb bay. I was never given a reason why they should be tied to the internal bomb racks, I was just told that it was an Air Ministry instruction.

The first week in January saw us receive our first mail from home. I believe I had a dozen or more letters and air mail letters from Mary. It was so good at last to have news of home, but there were disappointed faces amongst us who had no mail. That same week saw me finding a bed space in the permanent camp in the Armourer Barrack Block. I wasn't able to move into a room but had my charpoy (string bed) on the upper veranda. I was to find within the next 24 hours that the Karachi Barracks were alive with bed bugs. We had to keep the legs of our charpoys in tobacco or fruit tins filled with paraffin and keep the mosquito net away from the walls to try and keep the bugs getting on the bed. I am sure they crawled on to the ceiling and dropped onto the netting as there was no way we could stop them getting to bite us, and if we crushed them the smell was revolting! We also had our charpoys dipped in a paraffin bath every two weeks but to no avail.

It became necessary now for me to purchase a clay water pitcher to hold and keep cool drinking water. This was purchased for me by the Barrack Room Bearer (servant) and cost me about one rupee. This was kept full at all times by the Bearer, whose duties also included making up our beds, cleaning shoes, taking our laundry to the Dhobi Wallah (laundry) every day, and generally keeping the barrack room and adjacent veranda clean and protecting our belongings. This was a highly sought after position of trust, for which we paid him about 1 rupee each week; with about 30 men to a room and veranda, this was a small fortune to him.

I was called to the Station Armoury in mid-March and informed that I was being sent on a Bomb Disposal Course at the Royal Electrical and Mechanical Engineers School at Poona, and I was to be accompanied by a LAC Armourer from RAF Karachi Airport, which was a mile or so from Drigh Road. The course was to commence on March 22nd, for 14 days.

We left Drigh Road Railway Station early on March 19th, with a pack of sandwiches each for what was to be a three day journey. Our fist change of trains was at Hyderabad Sind, mid-morning where we joined the Jodhpur State narrow gauge railway and stayed with this train that day and the next, arriving at Ahmadabad about 2000hrs on March 20th. There we made our next change of trains and again travelled through the night, arriving at Bombay early morning of March 21st. After time for a meal of sorts in a forces canteen on the railway station, we caught the train to Poona.

From Hyderabad Sind we shared the compartment on the train all the way to Ahmadabad with two Dutch Jesuit priests who had been in India some years and very good travelling companions they turned out to be. They spoke English, Urdu and several Hindi dialects and made our journey so interesting, pointing out all the landmarks and temples, etc, en route and telling us some of the history attached to them. Of course we were quizzed about conditions in Britain and about the bombing and rationing, among other things, so the journey was far from boring.

They were also whist fanatics and had us make a foursome most of the two days and half of the night we were in their company. They also had a large cold box of food with them which they shared with us, the four of us only having to buy tea at the various stops the train made for connections or refreshments. Unfortunately our destinations were different and we parted company at Ahmadabad, but we had thoroughly enjoyed their company.

We were about 20 personnel on the course, just four of us from the Royal Air Force, the rest from different units of the army. The course was mostly classroom work with lectures on the workings and functions of the various types of German, Italian and Japanese bombs and mines and how to stop the clock delay mechanisms. We were given instructions on how to defuse the different types. We did have two days of digging and going through the motions of defusing, making safe and recovering some bombs that had been fused and buried as practical exercises. There was no examination as such at the end of the course, just a couple of questions and answers with the instructors.

It was back to Karachi on April 5th, another three day journey, stopping this time for a few hours in Bombay while we waited for a train. I bought a steel travelling trunk in the bazaar there (now in my grandson's possession), my kit bag was getting a bit worn, but more than that it was to protect my clothes etc from the white ants (termites) which could eat anything to their taste.

This time, back on No 320 MU I was to have an assistant to help me with all the examination after the assembly was completed. His name was Bill Simpson, a LAC, and he was a geology lecturer at Liverpool University prior to volunteering for the RAF at the outbreak of war. We got on well together and made a good team.

By this time I had made friends with another LAC, Benny Skitteral, a Londoner who had, prior to being called up, worked in the printing trade producing Police Gazettes. Benny had been in India about six months longer than me. Prior to being posted to No 320 MU he had been on a Coastal Command Squadron at Vizagapatam on the Eastern coast of India. Only on a few occasions did Benny and I work together, he being on the Test and Dispatch Flight, but we spent a lot of off-duty time in each other's company, especially on Saturdays when we visited Karachi for a Chinese meal and a trip to one of the cinemas. It was Benny who introduced me to chow mein, chop suey and various other Eastern dishes.

I recall one occasion when Ben came to me for assistance when he had an Avro Anson aircraft with a forward-firing Browning gun that would not fire after the first round whilst installed in the aircraft. Taken out it would fire perfectly on the butts, but back in the aircraft and out over the sea it would fire the first round already in the breech and then stop. Twice the pilot took us out over the sea to try and get the gun to fire but with negative results. I don't know what happened to it, it wasn't my responsibility.

Shortly after my return from Poona I managed to get myself a bed space and move into one of the rooms in the same barrack block on the posting of one of the armourers. Within days I had become one of a foursome in a solo whist school and we four played together from then until we were split up on posting at the end of that year. One of our foursome, a fellow from Burford in Oxfordshire, introduced the other three of us to what he called a 'Burford Emp', where after a shuffle and sorting, the cards were re-stacked and then 13 cards were dealt straight to each player instead of the orthodox deal of three and four cards to each player. We had great evening together.

It was sometime mid-1943 that there was an organised boycott of the main dining hall at RAF Drigh road, Karachi. This was by the whole of the station, Junior NCOs and other ranks and it was against the quality of the food served by the kitchen staff. I remember the boycott was for the midday meal only. I can still see the Orderly Officer, a young pilot officer (flying rank) standing on the steps of the hall pleading with the gathered personnel to enter, telling them of the meal on offer.

The four organisers of the boycott I understood were posted that same day from Karachi, but the quality of the food and the cooking of it improved 100% from that day on. Perhaps the cooks were posted as well, that I can't recall.

Sometime later that same year Spitfire Mk VIIIs and Hurricane Mk IIDs started arriving for assembly and to facilitate this a temporary wooden hanger was constructed by stacking the aircraft crates together, two high, and an assembly line created with a canvas roof. The Hurricanes Mk IIA, Mk IIB and Mk IIC assembly lines were then transferred to this new construction. The empty insides of the crates were used as workshops and offices. This allowed the assembly of the Spitfires and the Hurricanes Mk IIDs to be carried out in the main hangar.

These spitfire Mk VIIIs were the first I had seen and were armed with two 20 mm Hispano cannons, one each in the wing with a belt-feed mechanism that displaced the old 60 round magazine that we couldn't get to work on No 19 Squadron. These cannons were located where the inner Browning guns of the older Spitfires were located, but these Mk VIIIs also carried the four .303 Browning guns, two in each wing as in previous Mks.

The Hurricane Mk IID was armed with two 40 mm Vickers S guns, under-slung in a pod, one gun under each wing, and two .303 Browning guns in each wing, and came to be known after their success in the Middle East as 'Tank Busters'. We armourers at Drigh Road had some difficulty at first with these S guns, none of us had ever seen one before and there were no instruction manuals, so even stripping them was a matter of guesswork and making notes of every part we removed and in what sequence. I believe there was also provision under each wing of the Hurricane for the fitting of bomb racks, one on each side.

The months were rolling by and we heard and read daily of the progress of the war in other spheres of operations. We seemed so out of it all in our quiet corner of the world and apart from being so far from our loved ones we didn't feel as it we were at war with anyone. We all did look forward to having our mail from home but even this we received in batches. Christmas was only weeks away and we knew that there were to be a lot of seasonal festivities and we were to be allowed to construct a theme pub in each section, i.e. Armourers, Fight Mechs, Motor Transport section, etc, as in previous years and so we set about the Armourers Bar to be known as the 'Plumbers Arms', our pub being planned by one of our armourers, a gentleman from Kidderminster who was an architect in civilian life. It was to be constructed of wood, recovered from aircraft crates and cannon boxes, and sited outside the Armourers Barrack Block. I had no part in the building of the pub, it was all left to those armourers who were more adept with hammer, nails, saws, and paint brushes. But the finished building was a work the constructors could be proud of. The outside was of mock Tudor design with a black and white finish, the inside complementary to the outside and complete with an inglenook. The building won the C.O's prize, awarded each year for the best 'pub'. Other than 'The Wheelers', the Transport Section's entry, I have forgotten those entered by the other sections. I was told some years later, that in the late 1940s and before the RAF left India, that the Plumbers Arms had become a ladies club room for the wives of the RAF officers at Drigh Road.

Our Christmas in 1943 was much better than that of the previous year. Again there was Guinea Fowl but this time I had a share of it, and it was better than the corned beef of Christmas 1942! I think we had two days off-duty for the festivities, not that we needed any rest as none of us were hard worked because there were so many armourers on the station.

Early February 1944 I was informed that Percy Hemmings and I, along with about 20 other rank armourers were being posted to No 308 MU at Allahabad in the United Province of India. We were mostly from the Assembly Section. My friend Benny Skitteral was included in the postings. It was one of those 'here today, gone tomorrow' moves. In just 48 hours we were on our way.

Chapter Fifteen

NO 308 MAINTENANCE UNIT
RAR BAMRAULI
ALLAHABAD, INDIA

If I remember rightly, it was on my birthday that we moved, February 17th. We had a railway coach to ourselves from Drigh Road. The coach was standing in the siding at Drigh Road Railway Station where we entrained. We were supplied with several large cardboard boxes containing bread, tinned corned beef, tinned spam, tea, sugar and a couple of dozens tins of evaporated milk. We were also given a steel cauldron that would hold about four gallons of liquid, which was to enable us to make tea. The hot water was to be supplied by the train engine whenever we stopped long enough to make the run to and from the coach to the engine. I must say the stops were fairly regular and long, and our coach was not always at the rear of the train throughout our journey to Allahabad.

The coach was attached to the rear of a stopping train for the first part of our journey. This was to Hydrabad Sind where I changed trains and met the Jesuit priests on my journey to Poona. Here our coach was shunted into a siding and I was informed by the local station master that we were staying there for the night before being attached to a train the following morning to take us on our way to Delhi and Allahabad.

The Station Master warned us of thieves and advised me to appoint armed sentries outside the coach throughout the night and informed me that we could obtain hot water from the station to make tea and we could use the station toilet facilities to wash and shave. We were issued with a Sten gun each on leaving Karachi. I think this was a way of distributing the guns around India. We handed the guns into the armoury on arriving at our destination so there was no problem arming the chaps, but there was no way they could have shot anyone: we hadn't been issued with any ammunition!

What a journey, it was about four days and nights. I remember the bread was stale before we finished it and had to be thrown away, and once opened the tinned meat had to be eaten there and then because in minutes, if left unattended, it was covered with flies and contaminated. I think we started to buy food at the larger stations we stopped at after the second day.

No one at Allahabad Railway Station knew of us until I reported our arrival at Railway Transport Office (RTO), then a telephone call to RAF Bamrauli by the Military Police and two lorries were despatched to transport us the few miles to the airfield.

Prior to the war, Bamrauli airport was a staging post on the air route across India used by imperial Airways and was still a staging post used by the RAF as well as being the home of No 308 MU. I saw a lot of aircraft of various types land there for re-fuelling, including my first Lancaster, Stirling and Mosquito. The American Air Force also made frequent re-fuelling stops with fighter and bomber aircraft.

I had worn out my khaki drill trousers, shorts and tunic with which I had been issued at Wilmslow, long before I was posted from Karachi, and along with all my compatriots had replaced them with non-issue trousers, shorts and bush jacket made by the camp tailor at my own expense. Of course, everyone did this. The England issue of tropical uniform was more fitting for musical comedy and by the time I arrive at Bamrauli, the pith helmet I left England with was also dirty, battered and out of shape. This was replaced by an issued Australian bush hat (no corks!) and at the same time I was issued with a pair of British anti-snake boots. These were leather-footed with heavy sail cloth legs and were knee length, I suppose this was meant to protect against snake bikes. I can't remember if the hats and boots were issued at Bamrauli or Phaphamau, and I don't think I ever wore the boots.

No more pre-war comfortable brick barrack blocks. At Bamrauli, along with my fellow armourers I was billeted in a thatched roof hut but with no amenities of any sort, including lighting. We improvised with home made lamps. These were made out of Brylcream bottles or cigarette tins. We made a hole in the lid, threaded through a wick made from a piece of thick string or in my case a piece of pyjama cord and hey presto, a light of sorts. Paraffin was in plentiful supply.

Leisure facilities were non-existent. We did make a pilgrimage to Allahabad most Saturday evenings for a meal at a Chinese restaurant and a visit to the one cinema. There was nothing else to do. Back at camp our only entertainment was a portable gramophone, the property of the sergeant who had the small room at the end of our hut and he only had four records. I remember one vividly. It was Tchaikovsky's 'Capriccio Italien' and, by popular request, this was played over and over. Now, whenever I hear this piece of music I think of No 308 MU.

I don't know to this day why we were posted to No 308 MU, I can't remember doing much of anything there. The few armourers working under me and myself were detailed to carry out daily inspections on a few stored aircraft, including some Mohawks and Vultee Vengeance, for a few weeks, probably the same Vengeance that I had helped assemble at Karachi in 1943. It was during this spell that I fell ill. I was told that I collapsed unconscious on the wing of a Mohawk and slid off onto the ground. Fortunately I was not working on a Vengeance as falling from the much higher wing I might have broken my neck. Anyway I woke up in the sick quarters where I was confined for 10 days with dry pleurisy.

It was not a very pleasant sojourn, much worse than the chest pains was the smell that pervaded the building. Other than myself, all the other dozen or so airmen in the Sick Quarters were suffering with dysentery; often one or other of the poor fellows had the unfortunate and humiliating experience of not being able to get to the lavatory block which was in a separate building.

On discharge from the Sick Quarters, I was sent to work in the Station Armoury, or I should say, twiddle my thumbs, as there was nothing to do. I was completely bored. At the time I did so wish I could have got back on a Squadron or at least back on aircraft. The only job I really remember doing while being in the Armoury was being handed an American Signal pistol and about 500 cartridges and told to dispose of them. I took an armourer with me and we found a large drain or culvert that went under a part of the field and the end of the runway and got rid of the cartridges by firing them into the culvert, then burying the spent cartridge cases. The pistols and cartridges had been removed from American-made aircraft and had been replaced with British Very pistols.

While at Bamrauli, I remember a sergeant armourer in the Station Armoury, a Welshman like myself, and he was a very nice fellow, but he applied for and was commissioned. From the day he was commissioned he strutted about the Station with a peaked hat set at an 'Admiral Beatty' angle, looking for salutes and excuses to admonish airmen, or even to charge them with silly offences. He became hated and a laughing stock, even among his ex-sergeant colleagues. He was still at Bamrauli, awaiting posting when I left there.

I think it was in late April when I was told that I was posted, along with a dozen or so other armourers to No 352 MU at RAF Phaphamau, which was about 15 miles away and the other side of Allahabad. This time I was to leave all my old friends, including Percy Hemmings and Benny Skitteral behind. All the armourers going with me were strangers, no one had come with me from Karachi.

Chapter Sixteen

NO 352 MAINTENANCE UNIT
RAR PHAPHAMAU
ALLAHABAD, INDIA

It was just a short journey to Phaphamau, about 45 minutes by lorry. This was via Allahabad and over the Curzon Bridge spanning the River Ganges. This is a two-tier bridge, the railway underneath and the road directly over the top of the railway. It was queer as one neared the end of the bridge to see a train appearing from under the road!

Here at Phaphamau, like at Bamrauli, we were billeted in mud-brick walled and thatched huts. This time I was to share the N.C.Os' room at the end of the hut with another Corporal Armourer who moved from Bamrauli with me. His name was Bert Clinton, a native of Ludlow in Shropshire. Because of his stoutness he became known as 'Tubby'.

At Phaphamau, all the huts were built to form a square, each of four huts facing inwards. I can't remember how many formations of huts there were, and the formations were well scattered. We were all armourers in my hut and a few armourers shared a second hut in the square with other aircraft tradesmen. This second hut was in the charge of Corporal Alan Galton, the third Junior Armament N.C.O on the unit. Phaphamau was a new airfield, the hard standings were still being constructed when we arrived but the two runways were completed. The shorter runway was used as a hard standing for the storage of aircraft, there were perhaps a dozen B-24 Liberator heavy bombers stored on it at this time. This was to be my introduction to heavy bombers. Being new, the airfield had electricity, supplied from diesel generators, a big improvement on Bamrauli, and each square of four huts had a large ablution block with plenty of cold water showers and no water rationing. A small wood burning boiler with a capacity of about four gallons of water was supplied hot water to each hut for for shaving or other purposes.

There was an irrigation canal running through the camp that supplied the villages, there being about a dozen villages in the camp perimeter. There was also a main road running through the camp to Allahabad, neither the canal or the road was adjacent to the runways. We also had a railway and station on the camp boundary, both road and railway going to Allahabad via the Curzon Bridge.

The confluence of the Rivers Ganges and Jumna was only a few miles from the airfield and daily we were to witness the burial corteges of Hindu families carrying their dead along the main road, probably from scores of miles back, heading for the burning ghats on the riverside where the cremations took place.

It was early rising at Phaphamau, a mug of tea at the cookhouse, then transport to the runways and workshops where we commenced work at about 0430 hrs, our work places being a long way from the domestic quarters. We were transported back for breakfast at about 0800 hrs then back to work until noon when we finished, it being too hot to work inside the aircraft after that during the summer months. I can't remember how many armourers there were at No 352 MU, but there were three corporals, myself, Bert Clinton and Alan Galton, and we worked under Sergeant Shepherd. We had no Armament Officer.

At the Armoury on my first morning, I was told to work on the arrival Flight and was to have an armourer to assist me. The work entailed checking all the armament on the aircraft on their arrival, mostly from America, i.e. bomb sights, gun sights, gun turrets, bomb racks, etc. Also we working in cooperation with the electricians as everything on the Liberator was electrically operated. After a couple of months I was also to work on the Test and Dispatch Flight because most of the new planes arriving were going straight to the flights, where they were tropicalised and modified to meet RAF specifications. We also stored and serviced DC3 Douglas Dakota Transport aircraft and the occasional Vickers Warwick Coastal Command aircraft, but all the armourers had to do on the DC3s was to remove the American signal pistol from the aircraft and stick a British Very pistol in a pocket handy to the pilot. We did have one very early mark Liberator in storage that had no front gun turret but did have a free .50 Browning gun in the nose and a Boulton and Paul gun turret with four .303 Browning guns in the rear. I never saw this aircraft leave the ground while I was at Phaphamau.

Our off-duty hours were spent in the huts in the afternoons, reading or writing but mostly sleeping. Remember we were rising at about 0330 hrs. In the evening we played cards or Monopoly. Saturday evenings, I occasionally went into

Allahabad for a Chinese meal and a visit to the cinema. I was saving most of my money. I had to think of the home I intended to make with Mary when I returned to England.

Our mail was getting through fairly regularly by this time. It was one of the things we all looked forward to. We had one airman in our hut who couldn't read or write. He would come to either Tubby or myself to read his letters to him in the privacy of our room and Tubby would reply to them for him at his dictation.

By May and June the weather was really hotting up (and I thought Karachi was hot!), and we were told that as many personnel as possible that could be spared were to go on leave to Chakrata, a hill station in the Himalayas. I was to take charge of one of the parties to go. This meant about a 60 hour train and road journey there and the same back, with, I remember, about six days there. The train journey was from Allahabad to a place named Dehra Dun, then by road up into the mountains. There was very little to do at this hill station unless one was interested in hill walking. The camp was run by the army but I suppose the higher echelons of the RAF thought it was a change from the heat of the plains.

Back at Phaphamau, now to be greeted by my first Monsoon. I can't describe the density of the rain and this lasted for days on end. All our clothing was damp, our bedding wet, hut roofs leaked, there was mud everywhere. But one good thing that came with the rain, all of those of us that suffered from that dreadful itching rash known as prickly heat, which came with the hot weather, was to see it disappear within hours of getting our first wetting from the rain. Also during the monsoon, on switching on the lights in the huts in the evening, the huts were surrounded by hundreds, yes, hundreds of toads. Huge creatures, where they came from or where they went with daylight we were never to know. Fortunately they stayed on the edge of darkness and all we saw of them was their eyes glistening in the dark.

At Phaphamau another of my duties was to inspect all the aircraft on the storage runway every two or three days. A colleague and I did this with a flight mechanic airframe name Bill Toogood, and a flight mechanic engines whose name I have forgotten. During our inspection we always found time to listen to Radio Delhi (or was it Radio India?) on a radio set in one of the Liberators, to hear the news. We were doing this on June 6th, 1944, when we heard the newsreader say that the liberation of France had started. By the time we switched on, the invasion was well advanced so we couldn't get to spread the news around the station fast enough. Fortunately for us no questions were asked as to where we obtained the news. Tuning in on the aircraft radios wasn't actually permitted and was a punishable offence.

Aircraft were coming to us more frequently by June and July 1944. We always looked forward to Liberators and Dakotas coming to us direct from America and not via England, mostly crewed by Australian aircrew. When these arrived they always had a lot of tinned fruit and American K Ration packs issued in the United States as flying rations. And also several cartons of 200 American cigarettes. Lots of these goodies were often left in the aircraft or given to us by the crew when they left the planes, all of which we shared with our friends. The aircraft coming out from England, which included a few Liberators (second hand) only ever had a sack bag containing some packs of dry biscuits and tins of corned beef and never any cigarettes. These aircraft were flown by RAF ferry pilots who returned to England via Karachi from Phaphamau.

After being so busy at Karachi, my life was really boring, there being so little to do. I often used to spend time in the Station Armoury, helping with any modifications when needed. My busiest time was when a Liberator was to be checked before departure to a squadron, then I had to operationally test all the gun turrets, Consolidated nose and tail turrets, Sperry ventral ball turret and Glen Martin dorsal turret, and also check all ten .50 Browning guns, the bomb racks and bomb release mechanism.

November 1944, and Sergeant Shepherd and I managed to get some leave together. I can't remember how long but it must have been two weeks because we spent it in Ooticamund in Southern India. I still have the railway ticket. We had hoped to hitch a lift to Madras, we often had Liberators going there to Squadron at RAF St Thomas Mount, but no luck this particular time. I will always remember that train journey. We had to change trains at a place named Itarsi Junction. This meant spending the night on the railway station, the Madras train leaving about 0600 hrs the following morning. The military transport official, an army sergeant, directed us to a hut near the station where we were given a bed for the night.

We hadn't been on the beds very long when we and the other personnel sharing the hut found the beds were alive with bed bugs, perhaps 10 times as many on my bed alone as I had encountered to Karachi. We had been lying on the beds in shirts and shorts and had to strip off to clean ourselves and pick the horrid little things out of our clothing. We had no means of washing clothing on the railway station. We spent the rest of the night lying on the station platform.

Again at Nagpur railway station we had a little trouble when a railway official wanted to eject us from our compartment on the train to accommodate some Indian family, who we supposed had bribed him with baksheesh, but no way would we move. We didn't object to sharing the compartment, there was room for six passengers, but the family wanted us out. I don't know where the family went but we stayed where we were.

We had to change trains at Madras and another night journey to Metapalian, from where we were to travel on the last stage of our journey to Ootacamund on a narrow gauge rack railway up the mountain. Unfortunately, a few days earlier during a violent rainstorm, a portion of the track had been washed away and no trains were running, but after a couple of hours wait we were able to get a lift on an army lorry.

Ootacamund was a town built in an extinct volcano basin in the Nilgiri hills, it was a hill station for the English and Anglo-English population of Southern India and it was one of these exile families that we stayed our leave with on a bed and breakfast basis. What I remember most of 'Ooti', as it was called, was the smell of Eucalyptus. The town was surrounded by Eucalyptus trees and also the smell of Jasmine. It was a relaxing holiday. We wandered the woods and searched bazaars. We visited the local cinema a couple of time and saw some 10 year old films, and we tried to learn to play Mahjong with the people who boarded us.

Our return journey to Allahabad was without incident but we were exhausted and tired and dirty after the return journey; it was a train journey of about three days each way.

Christmas at Phaphamau 1944 was a pretty dull event after the celebrations at Karachi the previous year. We had a ration of two bottles of Cawnpore beer each. This was lukewarm and a Guinea Fowl dinner, which was very good. I am sure it was a lot better than that given to our lads up in the jungle in Burma. There was plenty of Indian-made gin that some of the lads had bought in the town and that was it. I didn't partake of any of the gin, it looked too rot-gut, besides I didn't like spirits.

Into the New Year, 1945, we were all following the news from home and saying that this year the war will be over and we can return home. I was still carrying out my inspections on Liberators and Dakotas and still signing serviceability forms but occasionally there was a little light relief from boredom. One morning we had a Liberator on the storage runway catch fire. Occasionally someone from the Flights was sent to the stored Liberators to take a part off one of the stored aircraft to bring another aircraft to serviceability status. When this was done a warning notice was always placed prominently in the cockpit listing the missing part or parts. On this occasion it wasn't done, and when the Flight Mechanic started up the engines on the weekly warm-up, aviation fuel flooded the engine and caught fire. In a few minutes the fuel tanks and the main planes were exploding. Those of us on the Storage Runway at the time managed to slow and move the two nearest Liberators clear in time to prevent them catching fire, and so limited the loss to one aircraft.

On another occasion, a Liberator was taking off about 0600 hrs with a full load of fuel, a crew of four Australian aircrew and about eight other aircrew as passengers, heading for Madras non-stop. Towards the end of the runway, just after lift off, the under carriage not yet retracted, the port wheel and the under carriage hit a contractors lorry that was illegally crossing the run way. There were two workmen standing behind the cab of the lorry. They and the driver were killed instantly and the lorry crashed.

The Liberator's undercarriage was smashed and couldn't be retracted, so the plane had to fly around the area of Phaphamau until, if I remember rightly, about 1500 hrs, using up fuel. The crew couldn't jettison the fuel over the land. Then the pilot made a marvellous landing on his starboard wheel and nose wheel, traversing three parts of the runway before the port wing dipped and dug into the grass edge of the runway. The plane swung onto the grass with no one injured and all damage confined to the port wing, airscrews and undercarriage.

With news of all the advances of the forces in Europe and the end of the war in Europe in sight, it was decided in February

1945, that our ration of two bottles of beer each month should be stored for any victory celebrations. A small building was allocated for this purpose and turned into an icehouse, the ice being brought from Allahabad and replenished as necessary. Also by this time we had started having American K rations issued as a supplement to our food. These came as breakfast, dinner or supper packages, so labelled, and each package contained tinned meat or cheese or egg, biscuits and three cigarettes, a book of matches and toilet paper.

We also started having some supplies of Australian goods in the canteen. Of these the favourite of we three armament corporals was to purchase a box of Kellogg's cornflakes, an extra large tin of Australian peaches and two tins of Carnation Milk. Empty the lot into one of our hand washing bowls, mix it all up, the share them out. The mixture was lovely.

Mango trees were to be found everywhere in the camp, these grew wild, the fruits were edible but small. In places the trees were quire close together and with other growth formed thickets. Early in 1945, a family of baboons, with youngsters, settled in one of these thickets. Being close to one of the pathways between the villages and our work area and domestic quarters, the animals became protective of their young and a menace to both the Indian villagers and to us and after one or two dangerous incidents, permission was granted, I think by the civil authorities, and they were shot by the same authority. About this same time there was an outbreak of cholera in one of the villages. This meant every one of us having to have a further cholera injection on top of the one we were given the previous year. The Civil Authorities were called in, the people were moved out of the village and the huts burned to the ground. These villages consisted of, at the most, 10 huts and perhaps the same number of families, it was a sad occurrence. These were people's homes, but it was a necessary action to stop the spread of the disease. Cholera is a terrible disease. Come May 8th, 1945, and the announcement that the war in Europe was over. It was designated VE Day and we were given the day off work. We were to celebrate in the dining hut that night. All went well until the evening and we were issued with our eight bottles of beer each, only to find that the bottles that had been stored from the previous months had gone sour and were undrinkable. I can't print what was said a the time, but we had the consolation that now with the war in Europe over we were nearer to returning home.

I lost my room mate Tubby Clinton at this time. He was posted somewhere in Burma, to a squadron. I did miss him, we had shared our room and had been good friends for over 12 months. A new corporal took his place, a fellow fresh out from England but it wasn't the same after Tubby left. This new chap didn't fit in with any of us in the hut and I never really made friends with him, he seemed to be what we called a 'loner'.

Sergeant Shepherd was posted around the same time as Tubby and that was a great loss to the Armament Section. He was a great organiser and a good armourer. To replace him we had an Armament Officer, a pilot officer (ground staff), fresh from England. I shouldn't say it but he was useless. One of the armourers found out from his mate in the orderly room that 12 months previous this new officer had been a tram driver in Blackpool. His father was an ex-mayor of Blackpool and had pulled strings somewhere and acquired him his commission. The Royal Air Force was very prominent in Blackpool throughout the war. His armament knowledge was negligible and he was suspicious of every bit of work we did. It was pretty well impossible to get him to sign for or to take responsibility for anything.

A few weeks before my time to return home, we had a sad occurrence. We had a tractor driver killed. He had just unhitched his tractor from the nose wheel of a Liberator after towing it to the hard standing, and was going to drive away, but unfortunately had the tractor in reverse gear; he reversed under the nose and front turret of the Liberator trapping him between the steering wheel and the nose of the aircraft, crushing him.

The work was running down, we were getting very few aircraft through and most those were planes taken out of service in Europe and diverted. Our war was certainly over at Allahabad, although I thought mine had finished when I left Karachi. Then came some news, I heard that Benny Skitteral had been posted home from Bamrauli some week's previous and Percy Hemmings, who travelled to India with me, had got his posting home and was leaving for Bombay that week. I was immediately over to the Orderly Room, wanting to know where my posting home was. The staff there had no knowledge of any posting home for me, but would make enquiries.

Two days later I was posted to Wholi transit camp at Bombay. I remember that our C.O and I were posted home on the same ship. I had six days in which to have all clearance chits etc, signed and hand over all tools and responsibilities.

I found , on asking for clearance from the Camp Dentist, that I had to have one back tooth taken out and several more filled before he would clear me. I think he made all this work because he was bored. On talking to me on the two visits I made to his surgery, we talked of Stratford-upon-Avon and he told me his home was in the Cotswolds. He only took up dentistry as a profession when a young man for something to do. To drill the cavities in my teeth he had a somewhat antiquated machine that had a foot treadle that he pedalled to drier the drill. He did warn me that his hand wasn't too steady I suffered in silence.

Now the nasty bit. The Armament Officer had asked me to instruct the men in the Armoury to make some perspex windows for his room at the Officers' Quarters to replace the wooden shutters already in place. This I refused to do as it would have been a misuse of material, and the men also refused. He couldn't charge us with anything but now, on my presenting him with my clearance chit to be signed, he refused, saying it would stop my posting. We had a few nasty words and I went and spoke to the C.O about this, knowing we were going home the same time. I don't know what was said between the C.O and the Armament Officer on the telephone but the latter arrived at the C.O's Office, red faced. The C.O himself signed my chit and I never saw the Armament Officer again.

Chapter Seventeen

HOMEWARD BOUND

It was an overnight journey from Allahabad to Bombay. I was travelling second class in one part of the train, the C.O first class in another. Transport was waiting at Bombay Railway Station to take us to Whorli Transit Camp outside Bombay. There I was accompanied to a large barrack building and told to find myself a bed, one of about 50 or more in this one large room.

In the following days, I handed in my snake boots, mosquito net, Sten gun and other items of kit that I wouldn't need in England. I made a couple of trips into Bombay to purchase some things for our future home such as towels, tablecloths, things that were rationed and could only be bought with coupons at home. Some other junior N.C.Os, also on draft home, and I were told we were to be in charge of an advance party to board ship the day prior to the remaining 2,000 or more time-expired men boarding, all homeward bound.

The ship was the *Capetown Castle* of the Union Castle Line. On boarding, a couple of the corporals and some of the airmen were given duties that entailed controlling the queues on the stairways to the dining hall at mealtimes. A further couple of corporals were given RAF Police armbands to wear but no instruction about what they were to police. The rest of us were dismissed as surplus.

I will always remember my first meal on board. It was tea time and apart from our advance party, a few civilians and some WAAFs there was only the ship's crew on board. We were given kippers, as many as we wanted, and as much fresh white bread and English butter as we could eat, the bread was baked on the ship. I don't think we had ever enjoyed a meal more than that one.

I can't remember the date we sailed from Bombay, but it was a straight sailing to England. No zigzag on this voyage and no escort. We returned via the Suez Canal, stopping at Port Said to pick up passengers. We were passing Malta late one evening on the voyage. The island was pointed out to us by a tannoy announcement, and we could see lights on the island. On this same evening we were told by the same tannoy system that the Americans had dropped the first atom bomb on Hiroshima in Japan.

We arrived in the firth of Clyde on August 14th, 1945, but the ship didn't dock until the next day when we disembarked and entrained and travelled to Morecambe, where we were boarded at various guest houses throughout the town.

That day, my first day back in England was to become known as 'VJ Day', the day the war with Japan ended, and this meant big celebrations everywhere. As we had just arrived back from the Far East everyone, and there were thousands of holiday makers in Morecambe at this time, wanted to buy us drinks. There was dancing on the promenade, congas on the pier, free entry to the theatres for us if we could get away from all the hospitality offered and towards midnight a tremendous bonfire on the beach. I don't know where all the combustibles came from but I remember well a lot of seats from the promenade burning well.

During the next few days we were issued with new uniforms, our old and only suit of blue becoming our working uniform. We were also issued with any deficiencies in our kit such as socks, caps, and under clothing. We had all discarded all our tropical clothes over the side of the ship on the voyage home, this on instruction. There was also the usual form filling and an advance of pay to collect, leave form 295s to get signed and railway station tickets to be acquired. I was to get three weeks leave, one for each year of overseas service.

We were highly entertained each night at Morecambe by both the holiday makers and by locals, but the few days we were at Morecambe soon passed and it was a train journey to Stratford-upon-Avon, changing trains at Birmingham and a taxi ride to Temple Grafton.

The three weeks leave passed all too quickly, there was only time to make a couple of visits to my parents in Neath and my grandmother in Swansea, who was terminally ill and died a few weeks later. I would like to think she lived only long enough to see me, me being her eldest and favourite grandchild.

During my leave I had the problem of finding my steel travelling trunk that followed me from Glasgow after we disembarked. I eventually found it at the little wayside railway station of Binton, near Mary's home village of Temple Grafton.

The railway cartage company hadn't delivered it because the cartage fee hadn't been paid at Glasgow. After I explained that I was a member of the armed forces and that I wasn't expected to pay, it was released to me.

I hadn't been many days on leave before my posting followed me, accompanied by a railway station warrant to Stranraer in Scotland. I was to report at the end of the leave to No 1 Marine Craft Training School (MCTS) at Kirkholm, near Stranraer. After three years abroad I couldn't have been posted much further than that from home in Great Britain. The people that arranged these postings must have had a queer sort of humour. Anyway what did I know about boats, it seemed so unfair, but there was nothing I could do about it until I reached Kirkholm.

Mary and I had so much to catch up on in this leave. We made a few visits to Stratford , empty now of RAF personnel, all the hotels returning to pre-war activities. We also did a lot of walking on our own and lots of talking and planning, then another farewell on Stratford Railway Station, just like the one three years before.

Chapter Eighteen

NO 1 MARINE CRAFT TRAINING SCHOOL
RAF KIRKHOM, SCOTLAND
&
RAF SNITTERFIELD

What a rail journey! I made an early start from Stratford-upon-Avon to Birmingham. From there it was a long, slow, journey to Dumfries in Scotland, then after a long wait for a connecting train, a longer, slower ride to Stranraer. The train stopped at all stations, halts and I am sure would have stopped for hitch-hikers. It was about a five-hour journey. We were two airmen and two airwomen in the compartment from Dumfries, all of us travelling to Stranraer. We had all been on leave, the other airman was a member of a Sunderland squadron based on Loch Ryan, and the two airwomen were based at Kirkholm. By the time we reached Stranraer at about 2200 hrs where we all alighted I was well versed on Royal Air Force Kirkholm.

On my arrival at RAF Kirkholm, which was based on the edge of Loch Ryan, I was conducted to a hut that was to be my home for the next few weeks. The whole of the station's buildings were of corrugated steel and wood construction, erected by, and for the American forces. The camp was situated just inside a large forest and being located in this environment the whole place was very damp; even in September it was very cold, the only heating provided by paraffin stoves. I felt the cold very much, having just returned from the summer temperatures of India.

I was also to find that the personnel of the station were used to having uninvited visitors to the huts. There was a large number of wild deer living in and around the forest but they were used to the presence of the personnel. The deer would come and peer into the huts over the ranch type doors. It was alarming the first time I saw two big eyes glaring at me in the middle of the night from the open door.

At the time I was at Kirkholm, the trainees at the school were all re-mustered redundant aircrew who had volunteered for Air Sea Rescue Service and being a training school there was very little for armourers to do. We were a staff of abut six airmen and two corporals, the only days of the week when work was carried out were Tuesdays and Thursdays when one of the pinnaces from the school towed redundant Sunderland aircraft from the adjoining Coastal Command station out to sea, towards Ailso Craig Rock, and sank them, the armourers supplying the gunfire.

I also had to do guard duties at Kirkholm. I think perhaps twice during my stay there. This was from 1800 hrs until 0600 hrs when I was in charge of the Station Guard, one of the duties listed for the N.C.O in charge was to enter the airwomen's huts to wake the Duty Cooks at about 0400 hrs in the morning. It was something like 'hut number six, second bed on the right or hut number eight, fifth bed on the left. It could be very embarrassing. I had to be sure they were fully awake and have them sign a Duty Book to acknowledge they had been woken.

The second or third day at Kirkholm I asked to see the Station Adjutant and at that interview pointed out that I had spent three years in the Far East and thought it unfair that I should be posted so far from home. I requested that something be done to allow me to be posted to perhaps RAF Wellesbourne or RAF Snitterfield, both of which were near to Stratford-upon-Avon. He agreed with me on this and likewise that there was little or no work for me at Kirkholm. He promised to investigate and try to arrange a posting. A few days later the Adjutant sent for me and I was told the matter of my posting was in hand and if I would make out a Form 295 I could have eight days leave with a rail warrant from after duty that coming Friday.

Back at Kirkholm, after a very enjoyable leave and a much quicker train journey than the first time. This time I travelled on the Irish boat train from Crewe station straight through to Stranraer harbour, although I stood in the corridor of the train most of the way. I reported to the Adjutant on my return and was told that things were looking brighter for me, especially since I had taken a letter back with me from Mary's doctor stating that Mary's health was suffering due to my extended absence after three year's posting in the Far East. I think the letter helped things along as shortly afterwards I was informed that I was posted to RAF Church Lawford, a FTS based near Rugby in Warwickshire, and I was to be attached to their satellite airfield at RAF Snitterfield, which was about six miles from Stratford-upon-Avon and about 10 miles from Temple Grafton where Mary lived.

I arrived at Rugby Railway Station about 0600 hrs on November 2nd, 1945, after an overnight journey from Stranraer, and was taken by road to RAF Church Lawford. After a breakfast and some form filling at the station headquarters I was transferred by road to RAF Snitterfield.

On reporting to Station Headquarters, I was told that there was only a small Armament Section at Snitterfield, the staff consisting of one corporal and one airman, these people I never met. The aircraft at the school were North American Harvards with no armament, so the Station didn't warrant a larger armament staff. I was also told to report to the C.O, Squadron Leader Papworth, who explained things to me and asked if I would take charge of a party of four Italian prisoners of war along with a motor driver and a Morris half-truck and carry out duties set by the Station Transport Officer. I was also instructed to fill out the necessary forms, as I was being allowed to live out of camp. This meant I could cycle from Temple Grafton to Snitterfield and back every day when on duty, a round trip of 20 miles.

I was soon at Mary's home that first evening by bus via Stratford-upon-Avon to break the good news and I was to travel to and from the airfield, the first few days using Mary's cycle then purchasing a new cycle for myself that weekend.

On taking up my new duties, I now resigned myself to the fact that my immediate days as an armourer were over and at that time gave no thought to future events. I was to learn that the motor driver I was to work with was name Eddie Jobson. He too lived out of camp and in civilian life had his name as landlord and mine host over the door of the 'Royal Oak', a very old inn at Alcester, the little town four miles from Mary's home.

Our duties consisted of, on certain days along with the prisoners, who were very nice people, collecting tin cans, bottles and any other salvage suitable for recycling from the Officers', Sergeants' and Airmen's Messes and some outposts around the perimeter of the base and take it all to the local Council Salvage Depot at Stratford-upon-Avon. On Tuesdays and Fridays we loaded up the empty beer barrels and crates of empty beer and stout bottles from the Officers' and Sergeants' Mess and made for Bird's, a bottling firm in Stratford, where we exchanged the empties for full bottles. We also picked up cigarettes for the Officers' and Sergeants' Mess as per their requirements. We did well at Bird's, usually Eddie and I were given a packet of 20 Players cigarettes each, *gratis*, on each visit and on one occasion we were given two packets each. The prisoners were also given a packet of 10 Woodbine cigarettes each per visit. From there we drove to the Flowers Brewery in Stratford and after unloading the empty barrels we went to the cellars, Eddie being in the trade and being the licensee of a Flowers inn himself, knew the procedure. There along with the cellar men we had the Italians load up the full barrels of beer, again as requirements, then all six of us were treated to a pint or two if we wanted it of Flowers Best Bitter Beer, this straight out of the pipe that filled the barrels.

Yes, I had some good times at Snitterfield, they were to be my last in the service that I had come to love, but came the day when I was told to report to the C.O's Office. There I was told that I was to be demobilised under the Class A Release Scheme, as I was time-expired. My seven years were up. I was interviewed by the C.O and asked if I would take the opportunity to sign on for a further term of service, but I remember telling the C.O that had I been a single person I would have gladly done so, but I was married and didn't think I could, perhaps, face another long posting away from my wife. I also told him that despite my exemplary service, on posting to South East Asia in 1942, I had missed out on all promotion, like the airman's song says, 'You'll get no promotion this side of the ocean', meaning overseas service. At times during the latter part of my overseas service I had to serve under and take orders from senior N.C.Os with half or less than half my service and experience who had been promoted to their rank prior to posting overseas, and I could see little chance of promotion in the future. Air Force personnel were being discharged not promoted, and I thought I could better myself outside the service.

There was more form filling and a discharge book to make out, then I was taken to RAF Church Lawford where I was given instructions and a rail warrant and told to report to No 1 Personnel Dispersal Centre at RAF Kirkham, near Preston on December 5th, 1945. There I handed in all my kit, other than the clothes I was wearing, and was issued with a civilian hat, raincoat, suit, shirts, socks, and shoes. My discharge book was completed. I signed for an advance of wages and a rail warrant to Stratford-upon-Avon. I was informed I was still liable to be recalled at any time. I was granted three months paid leave and finally discharged from the service on March 6th, 1946.

Bibliography

Anyone wishing to know more about 19 Squadron and Duxford during the Battle of Britain period should refer to the following works by Dilip Sarkar, all of which are to be re-printed by Victory Books in 2006: -

Spitfire Squadron: No 19 Squadron at War, 1939-41 (includes a re-print of Squadron Leader Brian Lane DFC's *Spitfire! The Experiences of a Fighter Pilot*), Air Research Publications, 1990.

A Few of the Many: Air War 1939-45, A Kaleidoscope of Memories, Ramrod Publications, 1995.

Bader's Duxford Fighters: The Big Wing Controversy, Ramrod Publications, 1997.

Battle of Britain: Last Look Back, Ramrod Publications, 2002.

Dilip's new book, *Spitfire: Courage & Sacrifice*, also includes a detailed account of the life and death of Squadron Leader Brian Lane DFC, C.O of 19 Squadron 1940-41.

To receive advance notification of our future releases and signing events, please provide your details for our mailing list.

Victory Books, PO Box 573, Worcester WR5 3WU, UK.
Tel: 07921 503105   Fax: 01905 767735.
www.victorybooks.co.uk   info@victorybooks.co.uk

Your Memories in Print?
Your Book Published?

Victory Books was founded in 2005 by successful and well-known independant author & publisher Dilip Sarkar MBE, and builds on the succes of his previous operation, Ramrod Publications (1992-2002). Just one year later, Victory Books is already a thriving partnership, now owned by the Sarkar and Cooper families, based in Worcester, UK, publishing books from many authors on a diverse range of subjects.

For example, concurrently with this book, Victory has released *Naked Ambition: My Quest to Row an Ocean*, by solo Atlantic rower Richard Wood, and Dilip's *Spitfire! Courage & Sacrifice*. 2006 will also see release of books such as Dr Bernard-Marie Dupont's paper on palliative care, and internationally renowned sculptor Kenneth Potts' book promoting his work.

Victory Books therefore invites submissions on any subject, from new or established authors, and can provide a bespoke service to suit each individual. Services offered range from general evaluation of material, editing, layout, print and bind, and often Victory Books will also deal with marketing, promotion and distribution on the author's behalf. For more information, please contact: -

Victory Books, PO Box 573, Worcester WR5 3RU, UK
Tel: 07921 503105   Fax: 01905 767735
www.VictoryBooks.co.uk   info@victorybooks.co.uk